An Asian Anthropologist in the South
Field Experiences with Blacks, Indians, and Whites

An Asian Anthropologist in the South

Field Experiences with Blacks, Indians, and Whites

by Choong Soon Kim

The University of Tennessee Press
Knoxville

Library of Congress Cataloging in Publication Data

Kim, Choong Soon, 1938–
　An Asian anthropologist in the South.
　Bibliography: p.
　Includes index.
　1. Southern States—Social life and customs.
2. Afro-Americans—Southern States.　3. Choctaw
Indians.　I. Title.
F216.2.K55　　975'.04　　76–49448
ISBN 0–87049–201–2

For Pyong-Choon Hahm, with Gratitude

Preface

The initial writing of an account of my field work with blacks, Indians, and whites took root in the fall of 1974 as I prepared for a special lecture before the faculty and students of the Department of Anthropology at The University of Tennessee, Knoxville. The audience responded positively, and discussion continued through the subsequent formal reception and lasted almost until midnight. As a result of such enthusiastic response, I was encouraged to organize the material gleaned from my experiences for publication as a single-volume book.

I hesitated to undertake such a project because my treatment would differ from traditional anthropological writings in that, heretofore, most anthropologists have recorded their findings in their native languages after completing their field work and returning to their homes. Instead, I would be writing in the language native to the people being studied while I was still in the field—something that, as far as I can tell, had never been done. However, upon weighing these facts and considering also that my attempt might prove too bold and ambitious, in the end I decided to write not only for the seasoned scholar but for the student anthropologist just beginning his field work.

In order for beginners in field work to avoid as many mistakes as possible, I have taken care to relate my mistakes and errors in judgment of the principles of anthropological field work in an honest and straightforward manner. Certainly, straightforward expression does not justify the presentation of distorted points of view, and I would hope that my realistic description does not unintentionally include them, particularly since most of my work was related to subcultural groups in American society. By its nature my field work was carried out in very small southern towns. And as elsewhere in the world, behavior patterns, beliefs, and cultural elements of southern rural people differ markedly from those of the urban dwellers. I have tried to uphold the dignity of southerners and have made an effort to conceal the identity of the individuals involved.

It is entirely possible that a good many southerners and a good many nonsoutherners might disagree with my impressions as presented here. In such case I can only ask whether any anthropologist or social scientist has ever been totally accurate in describing an alien culture or society. Of course, criticism is more than welcome, but it should be of an intellectual nature rather than an emotional argument.

I recognize that no scholarly work is the result of any one person's effort. This work could not have been successfully completed without the aid of a good many people and organizations.

To my parents, both of whom are no longer with me in this world, I owe an intellectual and emotional debt that can never be adequately expressed. My wife, Sang-Boon, offered constant encouragement during graduate school and has been a full-time partner in field work and in writing this book. My two sons Johng-Yun and Ho-Yun, both in their preteens, have fully understood the importance of scholarly work, and have allowed me to devote time rightly theirs to this work.

I am also indebted to my former teachers: Pyong-Choon Hahm, my mentor at Yonsei University Law School, Seoul, Korea, and currently the Korean ambassador to the United States, urged me to pursue advanced study in the United States. Robert S. Lancaster of The University of the South provided me with the opportunity to engage in graduate study at Emory University. Fred R. Crawford of Emory University encouraged me to switch my discipline from sociology to anthropology and assisted me in the process. And Wilfrid C. Bailey of The University of Georgia taught me anthropology and made possible my first field work with pulpwood workers in a South Georgia community. His criticism was most valuable in improving the final version of this book.

I owe special thanks to my colleague and good friend John H. Peterson, Jr., of Mississippi State University for his assistance in doing field work among the Choctaw Indians and also for his criticism of the manuscript which was far above the call of friendship. I am grateful for the criticisms made by William M. Bass, Larry C. Ingram, Clayburn L. Peeples, Ronald

N. Satz, and James E. Spears. I am indebted to the anonymous readers consulted by The University of Tennessee Press for constructive criticisms which materially improved this book. Special acknowledgment is given to my students David M. Byrn, who filled the roughest spots in reading the first draft of the manuscript word by word, and Judy L. Maynard, who checked the bibliography and each quotation for accuracy.

Field work described in this book was made possible by grants from the Pulpwood Harvesting Research Project and the Office of Education, U.S. Department of Health, Education, and Welfare. I have benefited greatly from the Department of Sociology and Anthropology, The University of Tennessee at Martin, for its strong support, and I wish to acknowledge with special appreciation the encouragement and assistance offered by Stanley B. Williams, chairman, and my other colleagues in the department.

I owe very special thanks to the southerners—blacks, Indians, and whites—for their hospitality and cooperation, without which this work could not have been accomplished.

CSK

Martin, Tennessee
Summer, 1976

Contents

An Asian Anthropologist in the South
Field Experiences with Blacks, Indians, and Whites

Prologue: Resocialization but Nonimmersion

When I arrived in American society ten years ago, I was neither a trained anthropologist nor had I achieved a reputation as a mature scholar of any profession. I came to begin the lengthy rite of passage, graduate studies, in the hope of becoming a respected scholar. The result has been extensive resocialization into yet another culture.

Indeed, in willy-nilly fashion, my contacts with other cultures had begun at an early age. As a citizen of Korea and because of its geopolitical importance, I endured the historic ordeals of the successive dominations of the small peninsula by China, Japan, and the United States. In fact, I had to learn a new foreign language whenever the source of domination changed in order to maintain my position in the Korean society.

I began by learning Chinese characters in order to appreciate our long-rooted family traditions based on Confucianism. Then during the Japanese occupation I went to a Japanese-run school for a while. Speaking Japanese was essential for one's survival under Japan's colonial rule. It was the only language Koreans were allowed to speak in public and quasi-public places. Thus I learned Japanese history, culture, and the spirit of their military aggressiveness. As the war neared its end, we school children had to collect various items for war material every afternoon. These items ranged from hay to brass dishes to chopsticks. I grew weary of school and eventually dropped out of the second grade in the Japanese-run elementary school.

After the war I went back to school. The new Korean educational system was copied after Western systems. I found even more Westernization when I went to Yonsei University Law School. Yonsei University was founded by American missionaries in 1885 and maintained the basic Judeo-Christian ethics. Again I had to face a different culture. Indeed, my educational career has been devoted primarily to learning other cultures instead of my own. For me, education has served as a transformer of culture rather than as a transmitter of it.

While in law school I found I was not particularly interested in pursuing a career as a practicing lawyer. Under the influence of my mentor, Pyong-Choon Hahm, in the law school, I entered the graduate school for further academic training. I was mainly interested in studying the compatibility of traditional Korean life with the new Korean legal system. A modern legal system was established by the Japanese during their occupation, so that there had long been a great gap between the traditional Korean way of life and the legal system.

In 1963, under the directorship of Hahm, Yonsei Law School received a research grant from the Asian Foundation to study the compatibility between traditional Korean customs and the current legal system. It was a project of nationwide scale. I participated in that project as one member of the four-man research team that collected the data. Being so involved, I traveled alone through most of the Korean native villages for eleven months, moving from village to village by every available mode of transportation—airplane, train, bus, taxi, bike, and by foot.[1]

Ironically, participating in that research project led to my farewell to law. Being impressed by my potential for carrying on field work in the remote rural villages, fishermen's islands, towns, and metropolitan centers, Hahm suggested that I undertake more graduate training in America, particularly in the area of methodology. I willingly accepted his advice because during the field work I had often been frustrated by weakness in methodology.

My decision to come to America precipitated several concerns in my mind. And, not knowing the ways of America, particularly the South, I could not dispel them very readily.

I did not know how to obtain admission to an American university. Fortunately, Hahm introduced me to an American friend, Robert S. Lancaster, who was a Fulbright scholar advising law school programs in Korea. Lancaster is a lawyer who has broad knowledge of various fields and was then the dean of Arts and Sciences at The University of the South, Sewanee, Tennessee. He was enthusiastic about helping me obtain admission. Through his efforts, I was finally accepted as a graduate student in the Department of Sociology and Anthropology at Emory University, Atlanta, Georgia, with a scholarship award. It was a joint department, with sociology as the host. As in most southern schools except the major state universities, the anthropology program was very limited.[2] This limitation did not bother me because at the time I did not know the difference between sociology and anthropology.

What did bother me was whether I should take the scholarship offer from Emory University or not, because of its location in the Deep South. My brother suggested that I not take it. He feared I would be an object of southern racial prejudice and discrimination. Generally, the American South was known to foreigners, certainly to the Koreans, to epitomize the "White Anglo-Saxon Protestant (WASP)." It was believed that a non-WASP individual would be the subject of racial segregation and discrimination in the South.

I consulted with several Yonsei faculty members who had been trained in America. I was not successful in finding anyone who was knowledgeable about the South and the southern universities. Most of them had attended schools located in the Pacific West or New England. They were not certain if racial prejudice in the South extended to Orientals but suggested that I not go unless I had no choice. Someone said, "I've heard only two good things about the South during my stay in America: beautiful girls and fine weather."

And so I became fearful and finally called Lancaster in order to hear his candid view of the racial perspectives in the South. He should know better than anyone since he was from the South. He had been born and reared in Virginia. Nevertheless, he had gone to the North for his education and returned to the South. Thus I felt he would have a fair view of the contemporary South. When I related my fears of being a nonwhite in the South, he was very positive about the South. He painted an overall picture of the city of Atlanta and the South as a whole.

My English was too poor to follow his rapid articulation thoroughly. He explained that the South would not be as bad as it was thought to be by outsiders. He said:

If you're looking for a big city, Atlanta will not be one. But, you'll be very happy to see the beauty of the city. My sister lives near there in a place called Athens, where the University of Georgia is located. I enjoy very much visiting that part of the country. Spring in Atlanta is just wonderful. Speaking for the southerners, they are the most warm and kindly Americans you could find. I assure you that you'll be all right.

He predicted that Atlanta would be larger than New York City within fifty years.[3] Indeed, many writers who have written about the South have shared the view that the South would become exciting and progressive.[4]

Knowing that I might not fully understand what he said, Lancaster put through a call to Hahm and reassured him that I would be all right in the South. Lancaster said that even if there was racial prejudice and discrimination in some rural towns, the atmosphere would be all right on campus and in the surrounding community. He also added that the South was undergoing significant change. With the assurances of Lancaster I disregarded the negative image of the South held by Koreans and decided to go to Emory after all.

On October 2, 1965, I stopped in San Francisco on my way to Atlanta, and visited some Korean friends. They rehearsed the negative images of the South and added some horror stories related to racial segregation. They genuinely tried to detain me. They were especially concerned about the quality of southern universities. They felt the southern universities were academically worse than the second-class Korean universities. And I would end up speaking a southern drawl. Their understanding of the South was similar to H. L. Mencken's description in 1920 that "And yet, for all its size and all its wealth and all the progress it babbles of, it is almost as sterile, artistically, intellectually, culturally, as the Sahara Desert."[5] The South, according to Mencken, has been ruled by poor whites, its religion usually "Baptist and Methodist barbarism," and its education close "to the Baptist seminary level."[6]

My friends in San Francisco were even critical of my scholarship and refused to congratulate me. They said that the southern universities were so far behind the national standard that they were desperate to improve their image by recruiting graduate students from abroad by giving away scholarships. Meanwhile, such schools could not adequately educate the sons and daughters of their own taxpayers.[7]

I was told that my plan for going to the South and attending a southern university was not wise in any respect. Some of my friends tried to find a job for me in San Francisco. Some offered me free room and board until I could support myself. Their sentiment against my going to the South was genuine. One seriously said, "You can't imagine what racial discrimination will be like unless you've had that experience. With your kind of temper, I don't think you'll finish your schooling there successfully. Even if you were patient enough to endure such discrimination and got your degree, I don't think any Korean university would be interested in recruiting you later."

The racial problems of the South were steadily sounding worse as I grew near to it. I began to wonder if Lancaster had simply not been aware of southern racial prejudice because he was a WASP and an insider. Although the fall quarter at Emory had started in the middle of September, I stayed a few more days in San Francisco than I had planned originally in order to make a final decision about whether I should go on to Atlanta or stay there. I was vulnerable to the influence of my Korean friends because I was in a stage of cultural shock. There was a great temptation to stay in San Francisco since there I at least had a few friends.

During my stay of several days in San Francisco, however, I was able to find a pattern among most of my friends there. They had not yet finished their studies, although they had been there for several years. None of them had scholarships, so they took odd jobs which caused poor grades and slowed progress toward their degrees. In turn, because of their poor grades, scholarships were out of reach. I realized if I stayed there, I would come to be like them. I had to go on to the South as scheduled for as long as my scholarship was secure no matter what hardships I would encounter there.

Then, by chance, I met a Korean businessman who had completed his education in a southern university. I sought his advice, asking many questions about the South and southern universities, telling him the information which I was given by my friends. He told me, "I don't know how close they are to you, but don't listen to whatever your friends like to tell you about the South. They don't know anything about the South. Probably, they have never been in the South at all. You see, if they had ever been enrolled in the southern schools, they wouldn't want to transfer to other parts of the nation. I'm sure they would like the South and southern schools." He also said that the quality of southern schools was not behind the national standard and perhaps was superior, although they have never attained national reputations. Honestly, his remarks were not well received by me, because as he was a graduate of a southern school, I thought his view was likely ethnocentric.

Although I was skeptical of his assessment of the quality of southern universities, I was very much impressed by his view of the southern racial situation. He said, "If you stay here in California, you may very well face strong racial prejudice against Orientals, since the immigrant communities are visible and sizeable."[8] According to his interpretation, the presence and absence of a certain minority group in a given region was an important variable for explaining the causes of racial prejudice and discrimination.[9] Whereas, because "the immigrant community was not a part of the southern scene,"[10] particularly an Oriental community, there would be no discrimination. Further, he made the remarkable comment that, "as long as the blacks are in the South, the less dark yellows will be all right."[11] I decided to go on to Georgia.

As I rode into downtown Atlanta around six o'clock in the morning from the airport, I saw only poor-looking blacks on the streets, mostly at bus stops. There were no whites in sight. It was an entirely different picture from San Francisco. Atlanta seemed a city of poor blacks. If this was the case, then I figured I had to worry about the blacks rather than the WASPs. As a stranger I did not know that those blacks got up early to ride the buses because many of them did not own cars, whereas most whites drove automobiles. The whites did not have to leave for work as early as the blacks did. I was mentally unprepared for dealing with blacks. I did not know how they would treat me, or how I should behave toward them.

My worries about blacks and their possible prejudice against me as an Oriental dissipated when I arrived at the Emory University campus. This was because there were virtually no blacks, except in service positions. Later, I found there was only one black student in my entire dormitory. He happened to be my suite-mate. Even on the first day of my arrival in the South, I observed a clear-cut color line between blacks and whites spatially in the city and socially by occupation. As soon as I met a Korean student enrolled at Emory, I asked him about the blacks in general and my suite-mate in particular. He answered simply, "Don't worry about the blacks. The blacks in the South are not as bad as you have been told."

Indeed, my suite-mate was very cordial and tried to assist me as much as he could. While I had limited contact with my white roommate carrying on very rudimentary conversations, such as "good morning" and "good night," the black suite-mate shared much of his time with me. He was very sympathetic, particularly with regard to my difficulty with English. He was very critical about the attitudes of white students toward English. He said,

"Don't be discouraged too much. You're doing very well. You see, if they would listen carefully when you speak, they could understand without any difficulty. But, they think they can't understand English spoken by a foreigner. So, it doesn't really matter how fluently or clearly you speak. It's their attitudes." However, even the departmental chairman did not think he could understand my English. The chairman would say "I beg your pardon" before I had even said anything if I may exaggerate somewhat.

I was so busy studying that I was unable to observe closely the activities of the community other than in the vicinity of the university. Since I stayed in a dormitory, I did not have many chances to make contact with southerners, except the ones whose occupations were related to the university. I was not mistreated by southerners in terms of racial prejudice. Now and then, in the department, I was treated differently than, say, a foreign student who came from Belgium. But each foreign student was treated differently according to the reputation of his or her nation. I did not think of this as a case of racial prejudice. If there had been a Japanese student in the department, for instance, he or she might well have been treated better or worse than I, although we would have belonged to the same racial group. Thus, I could not feel racial prejudice per se.

Ironically, I never felt discrimination by southerners, but rather by native Koreans, particularly administrators of Korean universities, when I sought employment after receiving my degrees. Although I came to realize the academic standards of southern schools were not low and indeed, were superior in some respects to institutions of greater prestige, my education there was a liability precluding my being hired by Korean universities and government agencies. Whenever the recruiting teams for the Korean government and universities came to American universities to interview Korean students, they usually visited either New England or the Midwest via the Pacific Coast. Their criteria for recruiting prospective candidates related less to an individual's qualifications than to the reputation of his or her school. Apparently, it is thought not to be worthwhile to recruit in the South.

After I received my doctoral degree, I applied for a position in the Department of Sociology at Yonsei University. They did not, at that time, have a full-time faculty member and were seeking a candidate among the Yonsei alumni to fill the position. In 1971, I wrote a letter of inquiry to the president of the university, who had been educated in New England. I never received any response from him. A year later, the position was filled by a graduate of a midwestern university. I was later told by a friend in the university that the president was not interested in me since I had been educated in southern universities. I feel certain that the former president of the university thought the quality of southern universities was indeed as poor as Mencken had described.[12]

Of course, the pattern of discrimination against the southern universities was not developed by the officials of Korean universities, by any means. Rather, it was created by the Americans themselves, particularly nonsoutherners. The northern universities seemed to look down on the southern universities. This impression was certainly substantiated when I applied to many schools throughout the nation for my doctoral work, after receiving my master's degree from Emory. I received favorable responses only from schools in the South and in the state of Hawaii. I came to realize that the pattern of discrimination against southern universities has long been a deep-rooted tradition in American society.

Before experiencing a nationwide shortage of teaching positions, good prospective college-level teachers who had been trained in the northern universities tended to avoid seeking employment in southern universities. Russell Middleton noted this trend in his study on "Racial Problems and the Recruitment of Academic Staff at Southern Colleges and Universities."[13] According to Middleton, among doctoral candidates, the South ranked fifth out of five regions (the Northeast, Far West, Middle West, Southwest, and South) as the place in which they would want to teach. Middleton observed that a majority "even of the native southerners are reluctant to teach in most of the southern states."[14] In fact, he found "the candidates at the southern university tend to be even more hostile to the Deep South than are the candidates at the non-southern universities."[15] If that was the case, I would think there would be no immediate solution for changing the images of nonsoutherners toward the southern universities, particularly foreigners.

However, recently there has been a strong indication that foreigners' images of the American South have been undergoing changes. This is certainly true for Orientals. The Korean population in Atlanta, for instance, was only 20 or so when I first came to the South in 1965. Recent estimates indicate that more than 2,000 Koreans reside in the greater Atlanta area. There are three Korean grocery stores, which are kept busy supplying the demands of their customers. This is but one of the many positive indications that the real South is quite different from its reputation outside.

I owe much to those southerners who introduced the real South to me throughout my last ten years. Former Secretary of Labor Frances Perkins (during Franklin D. Roosevelt's presidency) exaggerated when she stated that "southerners needed to start wearing shoes."[16] Her attitude is indicative of the attitudes of many nonsoutherners, which have seriously influenced the attitudes of foreigners as well. Having spent many years with all types of southerners throughout my field work, I cannot support her statement by either a broad or literal interpretation. It is regrettable when other foreign students who remain outside of the South come to understand the South as being a remote and backward region because of the fallacies created by nonsoutherners.

Nevertheless, the absence of racial discrimination or prejudice against me does not mean that my adjustments into an alien society with an alien culture have been easy. In the past ten years, I have faced the dual difficulty of learning the American culture, while at the same time pursuing my studies and doing field work on Americans.

In the middle of my first week at Emory, I stopped at a grocery store nearby and picked up a few cans of food having been told that this would be less expensive than dining in the university cafeteria. Before my meal, someone told me I had gotten dog food. I had not read the labels in the store, unaware that dog food could be stocked in a store with human food. In stark contrast, I come from a society where dog meat is eaten.

While still in the process of learning the oral part of the southern English dialect, I was invited to a dinner in the home of a wealthy family. Throughout the evening, the hostess kept talking about her "darling." I was anxious to meet her charming daughter. However, her darling turned out to be her pet female dog. Again, I was discovering a cultural barrier that exists between my own native culture and that of the host society. A real embarrassment came later due to misusage of my English vocabulary. As I was leaving after the dinner, I wished to express my appreciation to the hostess and said, "Thank you very much for your hostility," meaning, of course, *hospitality*. This must have astonished the hostess until she comprehended the adjustment problem of her foreign guest.

Any individual who has lived in an alien society and culture can understand my blunders. They resulted from resocialization, involving the abandonment of one's native culture for that of another. My early experiences in America indicated the future in that resocialization would be extremely difficult for me. As a child in Korea I found resocialization much easier and, of course, it was necessary in order to withstand the constant turmoil. Being introduced into an alien culture as an adult was a frustrating as well as a depressing experience. Rosalie Wax has suggested, however, that resocialization or secondary socialization might be necessary for adequate field work, even if it could not supply the field worker with the same understanding as the native.[17] She has further stated that "in participating as he observes, the field worker undergoes a secondary socialization (or resocialization) which allows him to perceive the major categories of objects of the culture and to understand the major types of relationships and interactions."[18]

The demands of anthropological field training go beyond resocialization. A skillful field worker should immerse himself in the native scene,[19] and become "physically and morally a part of the community."[20] Most of my fellow graduate students in the field methods courses appeared to believe that such immersion would not be difficult. They were all armchair anthropologists as graduate students then, living in the sheltered environment of academia. I was different in that I was already going through anthropological training in a real field setting as a participant and observer in an alien culture. Hence, I was already wondering whether such immersion was really possible.

Being a native Korean, I forcibly tried to immerse myself in the culture of the American South, particularly through formal schooling. Because of intensive resocialization effort, I came to believe that I was genuinely immersing myself in the culture of the American South. I thought I had become personally and socially involved in American community life. Not only was I developing relationships with acquaintances, colleagues, and friends in American society, but I was also beginning to lose touch with my native people. I was encouraged on occasions when I found myself understanding and laughing at American humor. I also became a true believer in the common sense notion that the longer an individual stays in an alien society the more likely he will be assimilated into it.

Now I realize my earlier conviction was an illusion. I have found that the longer I stay in the American South, the more definite becomes my sense of nonimmersion in its culture. Having obtained something of the understanding of an insider, I know immersion cannot be achieved by my will and determination alone. I have come to agree with Wax that "becoming a member of a society or culture of living people is always a joint process, involving numerous accommodations and adjustments by both the field worker and the people who accept him."[21]

Once I sought membership in a local civic club composed of middle-class whites. I thought this would provide a shortcut to becoming a middle-class member in the community and also enable me to observe the life-style of the middle-class white southerners. Since most of my field work associations were with lower-class subcultural groups, life in the middle class was relatively foreign to me. Becoming a member of the civic club was not difficult. One had only to pay the usual membership dues. As a new member of the club, on one occasion I was speaker for the regular luncheon meeting. That event was my first and my last participation in the club. I seldom had a chance to associate with other members, if at all. I was unable to participate in or observe the life of other members. Compared with the lower-class southerners, the middle-class southerners were so formal that free access by a foreigner was extremely difficult,[22] and I always felt alone in the company of other club members. Eventually, because I was only paying dues, I dropped my membership.

As the father of two sons, I am a member of the PTA in the community where I now live. However, I do not attend meetings because I know I am a temporary marginal resident who has no internalized plans for the community. I prefer to pay dues, hoping others will do the job to improve the educational milieu in the community. As a tongue-in-cheek member of the middle class, I have taught anthropology courses on one of the campuses of a state university for the past several years. I enjoy sharing my experiences with students and colleagues. However, I can appreciate the absurdity of my position when I read evaluations by students, such as one this past year saying that "I enjoyed your course very much, although this was the first time I have had a class under a colored foreign instructor."

My field work done in the American South did not help me become immersed in its culture either. Instead, in the field, I experienced a constant pressure to conform to the role expected of an Asian. Almost all of the southerners I studied during my field work expected me to behave as a foreigner. I do not think they had consciously constructed a model of what an Asian should be, but they had enough explicit notions to constitute a stereotype. For example, an Asian should have yellowish skin and straight black hair, be short and stocky, and wear eyeglasses. He must say "thank you" more than three times for every simple thing or event, even if it is not deserving of so much appreciation. He ought to be polite and humble in his manner. But more than anything else, he should not speak English fluently.

When I fulfilled the characteristics, given above, I was treated as a foreign guest in the American South, and my field work in southern communities was judged accordingly. Southerners would insist on taking me to my destination when I asked directions. They would carefully pronounce or even spell words when answering my questions. In contrast, when I failed to satisfy the aforementioned traits, I was no longer treated as 100 percent Asian and did not enjoy the privileges accorded a foreign guest. This knowledge reinforced me to behave in such a way that I could be identified as a typical Asian.[23]

During my stay in a pulpwood harvesting town, I met a third generation Japanese-American of whom I will relate more later. He told me about his experiences as an Asian descendant. Despite his Oriental appearance morphologically, he spoke English as fluently as a native and with American mannerisms. This resulted in no advantages for him in most southern towns, where they no longer treated him as a foreign guest but as a competitor.

I envision this book as an ethnography of a nonimmersed Asian ethnographer who has done his field work in the American South. It is not the view of an assimilated insider who is unaware of his own cultural pattern, even though I have resided here for ten years, but that of an outsider delineating the "innards" of the South. I have not intentionally searched for the sensational, fascinating, or entertaining episode. On the contrary, it is my belief that a realistic description of the trivia of my living with the natives as a field worker would give an intimate picture of my adjustment to an alien culture and, simultaneously perhaps, a realistic profile of an ethnography of my host culture, that of the American South.[24]

Undoubtedly, there are many Souths, yet the idea of the South persists. The South is too vast a region and represents too many different life patterns for me to pretend to know all its facets intimately.[25] The range of my field work is limited to communities in Georgia, Tennessee, and Mississippi. Those communities, which would be but tiny dots on a map of the South, are not necessarily representative of the South as a whole.

My delineation of the South may be a portrait of an elephant drawn by a blind man who has touched only the trunk of the elephant. Nevertheless, allusion can be made to the uniqueness of this book. It will present a rare anthropological perspective in describing the personal experiences of a nonwestern anthropologist who has done his field work in a part of the western world. The few personal accounts of field experiences have been descriptions by western anthropologists of the various alien peoples and cultures of nonwestern societies.[26] Also, contemporary American communities have traditionally been studied by Americans themselves,[27] the results of which have usually been as biased as Lewis Killian indicated:

As black writers have been preoccupied with the problems of their race, white southern writers have been intrigued by the mystique of their region. At the same time, many non-southern writers have been fascinated by white southerners and particularly by their faults.[28]

Hopefully, this book offers a more objective perspective of the American South.

I must admit, however, that, even if I have maintained objectivity, my understanding of the American South may be immature because I could not attain true immersion and become a participating insider. In many instances, I have not been able to observe certain customs and practices because the natives did not allow me to witness everything they did.

Yet, I recall in 1963, while researching the compatibility of traditional Korean life and the Korean legal system in rural villages, my field work suffered from the traditional Korean custom whereby females are to avoid strange men. When I was allowed to talk to a young female, her parents would hang a curtain between us, and an elder family member was always present. Since I was a Korean, the native villagers being studied expected me to conform to their norms because I belonged to the same culture. However, the custom did not apply to a foreign field worker. They assumed that the foreigner might not know the custom. This has been exemplified in the works of Cornelius Osgood[29] and Vincent Brandt.[30] Both of them conducted field work in Korea, yet they apparently did not suffer from the female avoidance custom as I did.

Hortense Powdermaker may have had more difficulties in crossing the racial boundary during her field work in a rural Mississippi community than I have had in a similar community in Mississippi. She has admitted that her field work in rural Mississippi was far more difficult and complex than the field work she did in the exotic cultures of alien societies. She commented, "True, I did not have to learn a new language and the community was a subsection of my culture with a known history. But I had to find my way and fit into a southern community which, even in the mid thirties, was characterized by the deep fears and anxieties of both Negroes and whites."[31] My access to each racial group was tolerated and relatively attention-free in contrast to the case of Powdermaker. This, too, would seem to indicate that field work being conducted in one's native society is not necessarily less of a hardship than that conducted in an alien society.

This book differs from other books about American society written by outsiders, several of which included the South. Particularly outstanding were those by the foreign social scientists, Alexis de Tocqueville,[32] James Bryce,[33] and Gunnar Myrdal,[34] all of whom are westerners. Their major intentions were to study the basic structure of American society and its overshadowing problems. If I may use the analogy of football, their roles were to sit with the crowd in the stands and watch the overall game in order to study the teamwork. My description in this book is neither a discussion of the structure of American society nor a revelation of its overshadowing problems. Rather, I have chosen to use an "isolated camera" moving around the ground viewing the action on the field to expose the hidden plays which often have been overshadowed by the overall game.

I begin with a description of my field experiences in South Georgia, where I studied the life patterns of the pulpwood workers. That was my first major field work as a professional anthropologist, living and working with blacks and whites in a small pulpwood-harvesting town on the Coastal Plain. During this field work, I was able to observe two major racial groups, blacks and whites. Following that portion, I relate my field experiences with a third racial group—the Choctaw Indians of West Tennessee. They are off-reservation, rural Indians. The Choctaws are a group of the original southerners who have lived in the South for generations, yet many previous works in this area have often excluded them as southerners. My field work with Choctaws eventually extended to East Central Mississippi, where the Choctaw Indian Reservation is located. The receptiveness that the Choctaw Indians displayed toward me, an Asian anthropologist, differed markedly from that of the blacks and whites. Thus my field work has included three major racial groups in the South.

In its conclusion, this book reflects the many responses of these three groups of southerners to an Asian anthropologist and his responses to them. Essentially, an attempt is made to depict the modern South and southerners as I have seen and met them.

Prior to relating my experiences, I must inform the reader that I have tried to protect the privacy and uphold the dignity of the individuals included in this book. For the privacy of the informants and individuals being studied, I have employed pseudonyms for the individuals and locations mentioned in this book. Even if a certain location or group of people is identifiable, I have tried my utmost to shield the personal identities. As exceptions to this principle, however, actual names of my teachers, Pyong-Choon Hahm, Robert S. Lancaster, and Wilfrid C. Bailey, and colleague, John H. Peterson, Jr., have been used after obtaining their personal approval to do so. Since they are neither the informants nor the individuals being studied, in my opinion, concealment in this case is unnecessary and futile.

And also, in narrative parts, limited and brief though the instances are, I have made no attempt to reproduce dialects. Although this differs, of course, from the way southerners speak, I have done so because my purpose in writing this book is not to demonstrate my ability to use southern colloquial English. Even if the imitation could be done without altering the original meaning, this might give the unfortunate and unintended impression that I am depicting the southerners as irrational, provincial, and uneducated. Further, I believe, upholding the dignity of "my people" whom I studied, even in their conversations, is far more important than the scholarship of this book.

1

Field Work among
Pulpwood Workers

One afternoon in the middle of January, 1970, when I was nearing completion of my doctoral coursework at the University of Georgia in Athens, my wife phoned me at my office. She informed me that our son, John, a three-year-old then, had thrown a rock at someone's car and broken the windshield. My first thought was of how I could pay for it, concluding that it would require at least half of my monthly scholarship. My wife proceeded to tell me that the incident had been initiated by other older children. But while the others had run, John had remained at the scene and gotten caught.

At the time, my family lived in a small apartment in a public housing district near the campus. I had noticed before that neighborhood children enjoyed ridiculing John. Such interaction among children is a typical phenomenon around public housing. He was younger and a different species in their eyes. Also, he was their only "toy." Most of their parents were unable to care for their children because they had to be away during the daytime. My wife had tried to keep John inside our apartment, but that was not an easy job. Whenever he heard the children playing outside, he hounded her like a "mad dog," wanting to join them and be a toy for them. At the time, he did not understand English well. Not comprehending their motivation nor knowing how to interpret their behavior, he did not feel bad. One time, they put him to work collecting Coke bottles to be redeemed at a grocery store. For his labor, he returned home with a piece of gum, exhausted and sick.

After talking with my wife, I began to figure how I might move my family out of public housing. I was so upset that moving was a more immediate concern than getting my doctorate in anthropology. Even more unsettling was the knowledge that we could not move because we could not afford housing elsewhere.

When I am deeply frustrated as on that day, I have a habit of recollecting the childhood teachings of my grandfather. He told me that if one had enough bad luck, he would have good luck soon. Of course, the reverse was also true. Since this has long been one of my beliefs, I usually do not show my emotions. Almost always I try to hold a position of moderation.

I checked my mailbox twice that afternoon hoping some good news might compensate for the bad luck. So, I sat in my office absent-mindedly, keeping my office door open toward the hallway. Almost everyone had left the building, but I did not want to return to the milieu of public housing while still frustrated and irritable. Suddenly, Wilfrid C. Bailey, my mentor, walked into my office with a big smile. He was very excited. I tried to conceal my despondent mood and appear optimistic.

Seeing a file folder in his hand, I gathered he was returning from a university meeting. He explained to me that there would be a possibility of getting funds for studying pulpwood workers. He wondered whether I would be interested in developing a project with him to be approved by the funding agency. My first reaction was not pleasure but amazement that the good news for which I had so anxiously waited had actually surfaced. However, I could not respond to him immediately, because I was unfamiliar with the research topic. Further, in all honesty, I was not mentally prepared to carry out any field work with that specific occupational group in the American South.

I began to think about what I would gain if I were to work on the project in terms of my anthropological knowledge, and what kind of contributions I could make working simply as a research assistant for the project. Finally, I concluded that participation in this project would be a good opportunity to study social and cultural phenomena of American society, the South in particular. In addition, the point of view of a nonwestern anthropologist doing field work in a part of the western world might prove useful to other anthropologists—particularly since only a few nonwestern anthropologists have ever done field work in the West. And there were other advantages: by participating in the proposed project, as Bailey suggested, I could use the data for my dissertation and, at the same time, draw upon the invaluable assistance of Bailey, whose early works were in the fields of rural sociology and applied anthropology.[1] Until then, although I was nearing preparation of my dissertation, I was very vague about my dissertation topic and the field work for it. I had assumed I would do field work in my native society in preparation for writing my master thesis, in which case, I could not expect much help from Bailey, whose area of specialization was far from it.

Despite this opportunity, however, I felt myself in happy agony. I was pleased by Bailey's faith in me, and I wanted very much to do the job, but I was afraid that I might not be able to meet his expectations. First of all, I did not have one of the prerequisites for such an enterprise, an automobile. There would be neither taxi services nor buslines to take me into the deep woods. Thus, my hopes of carrying out such a project were dimmed. Although Bailey is usually a very sensitive man to details, I do not believe that he had ever been aware that I did not have a car at that time. Since almost all of the graduate students in the department had automobiles, the matter simply never occurred to him.

Besides this practical problem, I was struggling with an inner conflict about applied anthropology—the practical utilization of anthropological knowledge. The project would involve contemporary affairs, which I had wanted to avoid if possible.[2] No matter how I might approach the pulpwood workers, the nature of the proposed study would definitely fall into the area of applied anthropology. As a result, I might be classified as an applied anthropologist, and enjoy less prestige, as George Foster has noted.[3] And what is more, since the fund would be granted by the pulpwood industry, I was apprehensive about the kind of results they would expect. Further, I wondered what they would do with the information that I would collect. My training had implied that it was not right for an anthropologist to interfere in the lives of people being studied. In all honesty, I must admit that I had not matured enough then to have a philosophy or moral or ethical guidelines for applied anthropology.

Remaining to be tested was the native southerners' receptiveness to an Asian anthropologist. That essential requirement for my anthropological field work was my main source of concern. If blacks and whites were not receptive, nothing could be done. In my view, Bailey was gambling. Such a project might fall apart because of my racial identity. I expressed my concern about this matter to him. He was very optimistic, as usual. He believed that my field work had begun when I prepared to come to America. After my arrival, I had spent much time learning English and living in the

South, and thus, had been doing field work virtually every minute. He thought of my position as neutral in the racial perspectives, which should enable me to alternate easily in observing blacks and whites in the South. Without hesitation, he asked me to prepare groundwork for a project.

I began to examine literature related to the proposed study. I did this step not only because it had been suggested by experienced field workers, but also because I was anxious to acquaint myself with American pulpwood workers. I checked major journals in social sciences focusing particular attention on the areas of rural sociology and applied anthropology, but I was not successful in finding a single article written about pulpwood workers. The major indexes in social sciences left out both pulpwood workers and forestry as a heading. On the other hand, *Forestry Abstract* omitted human factors as a category. The only available literature was on the recreational use of forests, forest-fire prevention, and cultural factors in forest conservation. When I asked Bailey whether he knew any sources of literature on the subject, he said there would be virtually no information. He introduced me to a forest economist in the School of Forest Resources at the University of Georgia, who had studied the economic aspect of the pulpwood industry in several Georgia communities.

When I called on him in his office, I got the immediate impression that he was as sharp as he looked. Considering his speedy English with strong aspirations, I wondered if he were a Yankee. When I inquired, he answered immediately, "I'm a foreigner like you." I still thought that he was probably referring to nonsouthern origin and that he was indeed a Yankee. I had heard many times that some northerners living in the South cynically designate themselves as foreigners. As though he could read my thoughts, he added, "I'm really a foreigner. I came from Canada." When I muttered, "It's not really a foreign country though," he almost got mad at my thoughtless mumbling and strongly protested my denial of Canadian sovereignty. I had made a serious mistake in my first contact with an outsider for the project. I learned an important lesson that an anthropologist should listen carefully and analyze, and fit the remarks into his own frame of reference without manifesting his views to others unless it is absolutely necessary.

He handed me several magazines, most of which introduced new machinery for pulpwood or sawlog production. I was disappointed, having expected some scholarly documents. The unprofessional attitudes of the magazines simply did not appeal to me. Besides, I was proposing to study the "human factors"—the workers, not "machines."

Many pictures shown in those magazines differed from my childhood memory about the workers who cut the trees and made paper. When I was a little child, my grandfather taught me how to write Chinese characters with a brush on special paper known as *changhojee* or Korean-made paper. During my writing practice, I became curious about how the paper was made. I was interested in the kind of people who made the paper and in knowing the skills they possessed. I plagued my grandfather with questions about the mysteries of papermaking. After tiring of answering my questions, he took me to the mill which my family owned. Some noble Korean families then had paper mills which produced for their domestic supply. The domestic consumption of paper among Korean families was considerable. Papers were pasted for the windows, ceilings, and walls. And also, thick oily paper was used for the floors of Korean housing.

My childhood memory of the Korean paper mill workers was in stark contrast to the American pulpwood workers. The pulpwood workers were not the same as the paper mill workers. When I as a child in Korea saw the mill workers, they cut the trees themselves. Most of all, as those pictures showed, the pulpwood workers appeared to be a sort of industrial worker using highly sophisticated machines instead of craftsmen using two-men saws, axes, and sickles as tools. There were pictures of heavy-loaded trucks instead of oxcarts. My fanciful knowledge about the pulpwood workers needed to be revised. Finally, I was able to understand the intention of the forest economist who handed me those magazines.

Later in our conversation we discussed mechanized harvesting and the innovation of new machinery. Finally, we got around to talking about the workers. The forest economist asked me, "If you study the workers, then, how can you justify getting funds from the industry?" This question was directly related to the ethics of applied anthropology. I was not well equipped to answer the question. Nevertheless, I gave the following analogy of an automobile mechanic and his car:

A good many mechanics drive relatively older models of cars than do other workers in similar income categories. This is my observation. I believe this is due to their mechanical knowledge which allows them to make maximum utilization of models of cars. Accordingly, if management knows workers better, they can improve the production on the one hand and increase profits while improving the lives of the workers on the other.

He seemed pleased with my analogy. However, I was not satisfied with the answer, especially the phrase "maximum utilization." It sounded as though I were planning to work for the industry to exploit the workers without considering their needs. I had meant to say that I wanted to find out how the industry could change or adjust to improve the lives of the workers. My participation in the project had begun with role conflict. I had no training in applied anthropology. In fact, my department did not offer any courses related to it. Yet, I was already facing the ethical problems associated with applied anthropology.[4] Regarding role conflict in graduate education in anthropology, Carole Hill states, and I agree, that "the fieldwork situation may cause an individual to undergo role conflict in regard to his ability or competence as an anthropologist and this conflict may be caused by either inadequate socialization or, perhaps, oversocialization into the ideology of the discipline."[5]

This role conflict intervened even in writing the proposal. When Bailey and I were writing the final phase of the proposal, we directed the emphasis to a study of the relation of community factors to the productivity of pulpwood harvesting crews. In this way, we could avoid the sensitive issues. The proposal was designed for carrying out anthropological field methods in a rural southern community where pulpwood harvesting activities were easily observable. We proposed to describe an ethnography of the pulpwood workers which would include descriptions of the community in which the workers lived, the pulpwood industry compared to other industries in the community, and a description of pulpwood workers as industrial workers in the community. Hence the nature of the project required much information about the community as well as the pulpwood industry. In fact, the workers spent only forty to sixty hours of their week in the woods. The rest of their time was spent in activities centered in their homes, communities, and other places apart from their work. Limiting the study to their work in the woods would give only a partial explanation of the workers' whole activities. We estimated that at least a full year would be required for the field work, including the preliminary contacts with the workers.

After submitting our proposal to the funding agency, a body of research organization supported by the funds of several paper companies to study improvements in pulpwood production, we were invited to a meeting of its advisory committee, which was a rather unusual procedure. Hence we did not know how we should prepare for the meeting. Since most of the committee members were trained in either natural sciences or engineering, I believed they would appreciate a visual aid instead of an abstract. Thus, I prepared a flow chart which would indicate the operational strategies of our proposal.

Prior to the meeting, we fell into discussions with several committee members and were able to anticipate the attitudes of some. One member of the committee seemed to understand anthropology as a discipline which dealt only with primitive people. He told us "we don't have any primitive people in the woods." Another, knowing that we were anthropologists, thought we had found an archaeological site in a company forest. He was rather excited and said he knew something about archaeology. An industrial psychologist who was a member looked as though he were planning to block participation by any social scientist other than himself. No lectures or books on anthropology can anticipate the procedures of such funding agencies. I began to understand why field researchers express confusion and resentment about the methods taught and learned in the classroom.[6]

At the beginning of our presentation, Bailey gave a lengthy explanation of the role of anthropology in studying contemporary societies and the contributions of applied anthropology. Our audience was attentive and seemed interested. My operational chart seemed to be helpful for their conceptualization of our proposal. But as we got into our proposal, some heated questions came from a few members. They did not understand why we had to include the study of the community. They were unable to understand the relationship between community and industry.

Those members who were critical of the proposal objected to three points. First, we would work too slowly since we allowed a full year for field work and several months for writing the final report. They figured it would probably take two years. Secondly, the terms we had used in the proposal and would be likely to use in the final report were too technical to be useful to the management of the industry. Certain terms that we had used in the proposal—for example, *crew*—were taboo for the industry. Finally, our approach was too sympathetic to the workers. Anthropological field methods, especially the participant-observation technique, were foreign to them. They wanted a quick survey about the workers drawing a definitive conclusion supported by statistics.

Despite the criticism, the majority of the members were attracted by our slow-but-cautious approach, because it was a new method for them. The conference with the committee lasted eight hours, including an hour lunch and a few short breaks, before we finally achieved an affirmative decision from the committee. Not many anthropologists but Bailey and myself would believe that a meeting lasted such extraordinarily long hours in considering a research project. On the way back from the meeting, neither Bailey nor I had enough energy left to celebrate our success in selling anthropology to the management of the pulpwood industry.

Owing to my lack of knowledge about the pulpwood industry and the workers, I devoted much of February, March, and April of 1970 to preliminary study. This was to enable me to gain basic knowledge about the workers and select a community for intensive field work later.[7] I was aware that this would be a critical phase for testing the receptiveness of rural southerners to an Asian anthropologist. This aspect of the project concerned me the most.

Since no previous work among pulpwood workers had been done by any anthropologist, I had no reference points while preparing for my first trip into the woods. I had read literature on field work in general and autobiographical recollections of field workers in particular.[8] This literature assisted me in understanding some basic roles of anthropologists in the field, but it did very little to help me grapple with the specific problems I would face during my field work. A major reason for this was the most field work experiences in the literature were based on non-Western societies and cultures. Also, they contained the views of Western anthropologists. Comparatively, my field work was to be done from an inverted perspective.

Ready or not, I could no longer be a naïve armchair graduate student in anthropology. I had to go into the woods and find out what field work was really like. While Bailey and I were writing the proposal, I was very confident about the field work. I thought I knew precisely what I was supposed to do. As the time came to go to the field, however, I felt different. I became uneasy and confused and worried about practical matters, such as what equipment would be appropriate in the field. Above all, I worried about my reception in the woods and how I could best contact the workers.

It was about ten o'clock on a Monday morning (February 23, 1970) when I arrived at a woodyard in Atkinsville, Georgia. That morning the warm Georgia weather felt springlike. It is not difficult to find the woodyards in southern towns. Usually the cords[9] of wood are stacked alongside the railroad tracks. I had no trouble locating the small, wooden frame office. To one side was the large weighing platform for "scaling (weighing)" the log trucks before and after unloading. I had hoped that a man at the woodyard could introduce me to a truck driver whom I could follow into the woods to meet some of the workers. But there was no one inside the office or about the woodyard. So, I sat on a stack of logs and waited. After about two hours had passed, I was beginning to fear that months of this kind of waiting around woodyards lay ahead of me.

Finally, a middle-aged scaleman with a toothpick in his mouth drove in. He shouted, "Hey, boy! What's up?" It was the first time I had been addressed "boy" since coming to America. He did not allow me a chance to introduce myself but proceeded to ask, "Are you [a] Jap?" I answered, "No." "Are you [a] Chinaman?" Again I answered, "No." He seemed dissatisfied with the nature of my answer. But, I was not used to saying "yes, sir" and "no, sir." He then asked sullenly, "Hell, what are ya then?" I realized that even if I told him my nationality it would not help very much. I almost lost my confidence. But having waited so long, I decided to ask his assistance regardless of the results. Even if he would not be cooperative, I had nothing to lose. Explaining that I was a graduate student helping my professor with a study of pulpwood workers, I then specifically asked for his assistance. Instead of answering, he showed surprise and asked, "Y' mean yuh a college kid?" He apparently thought I was too young to be in college. He then said pointedly, "Yuh got a dumb teacher. Who's gonna find a good logger on Monday?" He meant that most pulpwood workers have a good time during the weekend and stay at their homes on Monday to recover. That was why no truck or workers had come by, although it was after the lunch hour.

This first contact at the Atkinsville woodyard was unproductive and discouraged me very much. I thought about attempting to make contact at another woodyard that day but decided against it. My feelings were hurt by the scaleman. Also, Monday was not a good day for contacting woodyards as the scaleman had said. I went home and began analyzing the language which the scaleman used in the woodyard. The way in which he called me "boy" bothered me. I figured it was not only because of my boyish features but also had something to do with other matters as well, perhaps my hair and clothing style. Knowing that rural southerners were not particularly in favor of the long hair style becoming popular on university campuses then, I had cut my hair quite short so that I might be associated with their tanned "rednecks." Further, my mode of clothing might have been a factor. I had worn plain pants and a jacket over my shirt thinking such dress would be similar to that of the wood workers. In reassessing, I felt I might be wrong. Certainly, the reaction was not what I had expected. Now I got the impression that I should be different from them. If I wanted to be identified as a graduate student, my identity should be recognizably closer to the group to which I belonged.

So far very little is known about the effects of anthropologists' clothing on their field work. When Pertti Pelto addressed the problem, he was very cautious and would not advise any particular style for any given field circumstance. He noted that:

When we consider that in every human society styles of clothing are important signals of social status and role, it follows that the fieldworker can always influence local attitudes toward him by adopting particular habits of costume. At first thought we would be tempted to conclude that the anthropologist should dress "like everyone else in the village."[10]

This must be the case I thought.

As Pelto suggested while studying urban culture, "in some situations (e.g., door-to-door interview work) it is important to signal a certain measure of prestige and status by wearing coat and tie."[11] Also, I felt I needed to wait until my hair grew longer before making any more contacts. For the next several weeks, I traveled to almost all woodyards in the Piedmont area of Georgia. I made up my own map of woodyards, indicating the size and prosperity of each. By this chart, for instance, I could distinguish that the Atkinsville woodyard was one of the smallest ones in the Piedmont.

My hair had grown a little longer when I visited a woodyard in Bobville, Georgia, on a Friday afternoon. I was wearing a coat and tie. My shoes were shined. I even brought my overcoat with me, although the weather was quite warm. I stopped by the office and introduced myself to the scaleman as a doctoral candidate and research associate at the university working for a research project funded by the paper companies. The scaleman's immediate reaction was "yes, sir." He introduced me to his boss, Allen Campbell. Campbell said that his close friend, Bill Freeman, who was a producer,[12] had a good crew that might interest me. As a matter of fact, Freeman's truck driver was in the woodyard at the time. Campbell called to the truck driver and told him, "Sammy! Tell Mr. Freeman that I sent this gentleman." Sam's reply was "yes, sir," of course.

I became interested in this manner of using personal names. To the black driver, Campbell had used his first name. When he spoke of Sam's boss to Sam, he emphasized "Mr.," although Campbell and Freeman appeared to be close friends. When Campbell introduced Sam to me, however, he did not mention his last name. I asked the scaleman what Sam's last name was. He said, "Uh . . . just Sam. Call him Sam. That's just fine." It seemed to me that nobody in that office knew Sam's last name. Until then, I had understood that only close friends addressed each other with personal names. However, I learned that this was not always the case when any black laborer was involved. When I asked his last name, Sam said "Hill is mine . . . but, yo' know wha'? Not many white folks know it."

I was set to follow his truck in my Dodge, but Sam lingered. I asked him, "Is anything wrong, Mr. Hill?" He was surprised to hear someone call him "Mr." and did not know how to react. I suggested that we go on to the woods, but still he hesitated. I did not know why until my Dodge got stuck twice in the mud on the way to the woods. It barely came out with his help each time. My shiny shoes were covered with mud. When Sam and I got into the woods, he did not look happy because of the wasted time and labor. He seemed to sneer at my clothing style which looked ridiculous to him under the circumstances. Sam pointed out Freeman with a nod and said nothing.

Freeman was a middle-aged white and very friendly. When I explained to him about my study, his initial reaction was sympathetic, yet he remained skeptical. Discovering that I was a Korean, he told me about his experiences in the East, mostly around Japan. Having been stationed in Japan after World War II, he tried to recall a few Japanese words. Soon, I became relaxed while talking with him. If I was interested in his crew, he was willing to assist me in my study. However, I faced some practical problems. For instance, his site was so low in elevation that the road conditions would almost always be bad. I had experienced enough of that already. I could not easily come in and out with my small Dodge. I would need a vehicle with a four-wheel drive—something I could not afford. Furthermore, as soon as the farming season started, according to Freeman, the entire crew would be gone for farming.

My observations that day with Freeman's crew included realizing some further difficulties in carrying out field work in the woods. For instance, in order to interview the workers I would almost have to interfere with their work. They were so busy during the working hours that I could not speak to them. During the lunch hour, they ate a quick lunch then took a brief nap. I realized that there were two possible options. I would either have to visit them in their homes during off-working hours and weekends or actively participate at the working site with the workers during their regular working hours. For the latter, my coat-and-tie clothing style was inconvenient. Already, it had failed one test when my car became stuck in the muddy road. Further, it was not sufficient to meet the minimum safety standards for the wood workers. For instance, when they took off the branches of limbs, I kept away because I had no hard hat. Yet my clothing had worked well in the woodyard.

For technical equipment, many experienced field workers recommend that one be equipped with a tape recorder, a camera, a battery-operated record player, musical tapes, and so on.[13] But for this project it was seriously doubtful that a tape recorder, for instance, would be useful for interviewing the pulpwood workers in the woods. My question about the use of a tape recorder had nothing to do with an assumption that the pulpwood workers might be suspicious about it. In fact, the use of a tape recorder among the researchers in the South, both in rural and in urban communities, is rather common practice.

My hesitation to use a tape recorder was based on my field circumstance. The noise of chain-saws and other machinery in the woods would interrupt the recording. And most of all, to be candid, I myself was very reluctant to record my own conversations. Because, it was and still is very embarrassing for me to hear my own strange accents and awkward expressions when replayed for reproduction. I have always regretted and complained to myself that I could not converse in English as elegantly and fluently as the native speakers.

I wondered whether many western anthropologists have been ashamed of not speaking the native language as well as the natives when they were studying in nonwestern societies. I decided to reproduce all the conversa-

tions immediately after each interview from memory as Powdermaker did
in the 1930s when she studied a Mississippi community.[14] I had to make
my preparations about what would be fitting for my work in the woods.

I busily made my preparations for the field. I bought a first-aid kit
having discovered that Freeman's crew did not have one. I bought a pair of
boots for the muddy woods and to protect me from snake bites. I obtained a
hard hat from the funding agency. I placed my camera in my car trunk, so
that it could be used when needed. I hung my coat and tie in my car for the
contacts with the front office. In this way, I could easily adjust my mode of
dress while alternating between the front office and the woods. I did not
forget to buy a small water jug. On my original visit with Freeman's crew, I
had gotten very thirsty but their water jug had only enough to meet their
own needs.

When I set out for another trip to the woods, my son was excited upon
seeing my hard hat and wanted to know if I had gotten a job in a
construction company like other fathers of his peers in the public housing
district. He seemed very proud of my being a worker rather than a student.
On this trip, I was thinking of contacting the workers in dual settings, the
woods as members of a pulpwood crew and their homes as community
members. I chose a woodyard in Bakersville, Georgia, which was owned by
one of the companies sponsoring the project. My reception was formal but
not hostile. I was dressed with coat and tie and carried my hard hat with me
when I came into the office. It seemed to me that they were very impressed
by the hard hat. I found out when I was introducing myself that they
thought I was on the staff of a paper company because my hard hat was
marked with the company insignia.

I was introduced to Bill, a black truck driver, who appeared to be over
fifty years old. As in the previous case, his last name was not mentioned. To
see Bill's reaction, I called him Bill without asking his last name. It did not
seem to bother him any. Taking off my coat and tie, I asked Bill about the
road condition to the site and mentioned my preparations. He did not think
I needed any boots. The route was a good one along a gravel road. The site
where Bill's crew was working was located on a beautiful hilltop. The crew
consisted of two whites and four blacks, including Bill.

When we got to the site, Bill went to work without introducing me to
his boss. I had not wanted to approach him without a formal introduction. I
decided to wait until they took a break, because I had been told as a part of

my training that a professional anthropologist should be extremely patient in the field. But they never took a break and worked until their lunch hour. Since both whites were busy operating the skidder (a machine which pulls harvested trees for loading) and tractor, I did not know which one was the producer.

Throughout the several hours I waited, they ignored my presence. This behavior was an interesting phenomenon and perhaps the most crucial matter to influence my study. I began to wonder about their unconcern about my presence in the woods while they were harvesting trees. Even a primitive people like the Lesu, who were Stone-Age Melanesian villagers, showed curiosity when Powdermaker went into their village. Describing the initial scene, she said, "almost everyone in the village was in and around the home gazing with wonder, admiration, or amusement."[15] But I found myself to be a lone Asian unable to attract the workers' attention. Sitting there in the woods, I began to ask myself why I was dedicating a part of my life to study the wood workers' cause and wondered what on earth I was doing all alone in the middle of that luxuriant southern forest.

During the lunch hour, the two whites took lunch together behind a pick-up truck while the blacks took separate places some distance away. In this way, each party could enjoy its own version of conversation. I hesitated for a while to see whether I should contact the blacks first or the whites. If I were to emphasize the whites, the blacks would think that I was biased against blacks, and if I gave priority to the blacks, the whites might wonder about my role. But I did not have much choice because Max Jones, producer of the crew, was white. I needed Jones's permission. As soon as the whites finished their lunch, I approached them and introduced myself. Both of them were Joneses, and I was to find out later that they were brothers. I explained my study in a cordial manner; nevertheless, they did not express interest in it. Their attitudes were sullen. I knew that they needed rest badly and did not wish to answer the questions of a stranger. Since they were part of the crew, they would like to avoid me as much as they possibly could.

After this, I asked for their cooperation in a different way. I mentioned that I was interested in the work habits of the black workers. Realizing this request would exclude themselves, they altered their frozen atmosphere a little bit. They asked me about my nationality for the first time. They then told me that there was a Korean woman in their community who had married a former G.I. while he was stationed in Korea. I expressed my eagerness to meet her. Max Jones suggested that he would arrange for me to meet her that weekend. I thought it would be an excellent chance to talk to him about himself and his crew. He drew a detailed map showing how to get to his home, but said that any one in Harmontown could tell me the way. It sounded as if the Joneses were very well known in the community.

When I asked his permission for access to his black workers, his facial expression indicated that was no problem. I did not bother asking him to introduce me to them. I preferred no introduction. Since he was a white boss, his introduction might create unnecessary speculations by the black workers. Also, I wanted the assistance of the black workers to learn about the white boss, his brother, and the overall relationships between whites and blacks.

My introduction to the black workers was similar to the former one. I only reversed the emphasis on whites instead of blacks. Bill complained sullenly, "How we gonna talk about 'em here, man?" All of them preferred to talk about the Joneses somewhere else and at some other time. Bill suggested that I drive back to the Bakersville woodyard. He would meet me when he hauled the next load. Everybody nodded their agreement to Bill's suggestion. Then, I thought, I could arrange the meeting with others through Bill if he were cooperative.

I had to figure out how to reach the Bakersville woodyard alone. I had just followed Bill's truck previously so I did not really know how to get back. In the woods, there were no road signs whatsoever. I lost my direction several times. I realized that in the future I would need a detailed map of each county and a compass. My field equipment was still incomplete.

In the woodyard, Bill was eager to talk with me about the white boss, but it was too late in the day for lengthy discussion. Further, there were so many whites around that we could not find an appropriate place. I sat with Bill in his truck seat and carried on a casual chat for a while. I made an appointment with him to continue our discussion at his home on Sunday following the day of my visit to Jones's home. According to Bill, his home was not far from that of Jones.

The day of the appointment with Jones at his Harmontown home was a fine, beautiful day with the typical early spring weather of Georgia that I love. Nevertheless, I was more tense than excited about the impending visit. Already, I had been told much about Harmontown from one of my sociology teachers at the university who previously had conducted a sociological survey of the county. He had given me many precautions about drunken fellows and bootleggers, particularly on the weekends. Harmontown was well known as one of the tough communities in Georgia for shooting, gambling, and fighting. Moonshine was another item which contributed to its bad reputation.

When I arrived in Harmontown, I stopped by a liquor store to ask the location of Jones's house. I was very surprised to find the store packed with customers. I began to wonder about the community function of moonshine since there were so many people in the liquor store. I wondered how many pulpwood workers were there among the crowd. Undoubtedly, the one liquor store was not sufficient to meet the consumption of whiskey in that community.

Following the instructions given by a whiskey customer, I easily found Jones's house. It was a huge, two-story, colonial-style, white, wood-frame house. It was too grand to be a pulpwood producer's home. It looked like an old plantation owner's house. I wondered to myself whether it was the right place. I was assured by the fact that the mailbox clearly showed his name. Afraid to drive into the yard, I stopped my car alongside the driveway and attempted to walk up to the house. Suddenly three big dogs came at me barking loudly. I stood still and waited for someone to come out and see me. As I approached nearer, the dogs became more ferocious. Yet, no one showed up. The dogs kept on barking. I was in an embarrassing situation. Noticing the unusual noise, Jones's neighbors came out, one by one. Seeing a total stranger, they stood still and gazed at me with obvious surprise and suspicion. Children shouted, "Come on, see the Chinaman," calling to their peers. I was no longer the attention-free man I had been earlier in the woods when they had ignored my presence. This was, I felt at that moment, certainly worse than the apathy in the woods. I impatiently wished for someone to come by and rescue me from the noisy dogs. Then, I could explain my business. But no one did so.

After a while, the other Jones brother, Bob, who lived near there, came by, heard the commotion, and saw the scene. I was so glad to see him that I almost felt like weeping. But he was not friendly at all. However, being assured that I was an acquaintance of the Jones family, he bade the dogs to stop barking at me, and the crowd gradually disappeared.

The most surprising thing was that Bob Jones and I found Max Jones working on his pick-up truck in his backyard. There was no way he could not have heard the noise from such a short distance. It was an awesome experience. He obviously felt awkward having me visit on the weekend. He blushed quite a bit. He gave no words of greeting even though I did, and no handshakes were exchanged between us. Simply, he told his younger brother, "Take 'im to Larry's place." Larry was the husband of the Korean woman. I had been totally rejected by Max. I could not choose appropriate words to say to him. I did not have any chance to ask either about himself or his black workers. I just followed his brother to meet Larry and his Korean wife.

Larry was casual and easy to associate with. He was proud, especially of his travels, and considered himself cosmopolitan. His wife was very glad to see a fellow countryman. She acted as if she were meeting her own brother. Indeed, Larry behaved much like my own brother-in-law. While Larry and I enjoyed talking about Korea and his rapport with Koreans, Bob Jones disappeared. Because of Larry's unconventionally personable character, I soon felt he was a close friend.

While his wife was preparing dinner, I told Larry about the cold reception of the Jones brothers. He was stunned and concerned about my welfare. Then, he commented, "Max is the meanest redneck in town." He told me more about the Jones family. The Jones brothers were the grandsons of a former cotton plantation owner. The family had owned almost a quarter of the whole county. With the fall of the old plantation system and the rise of a new middle class, the Joneses felt threatened by the community. In addition to this, both of the Jones boys were high school dropouts, and so they could not get good jobs anywhere else. Much frustration had been built into them as was reflected in their ill-natured personalities. Still, they owned some forested land, even though, according to Larry, the forest would soon be depleted.

When dinner was over, I offered to buy Larry a glass of whiskey in the liquor store which had a small bar. I was interested in seeing the night scene of the store. I knew I would arouse less suspicion and be safer if Larry would go with me. Larry introduced me to the storekeeper. Now and then, I had a chance to ask him questions. When I asked whether there had been any pulpwood workers in during the evening, he replied, "Are you kidding?" He meant there had been many. I asked him about the black loggers. The storekeeper showed me a pistol hidden under his table and said, "This's for them in case somethin' happens." I understood why the community had such a bad reputation. Larry and I did not want to stay in the store much longer with night coming on.

I told Larry before we left that I was going to visit Bill, a black truck driver from Jones's crew, the next day. Everybody seemed to know Bill and where he lived. He was known for his weekend behavior. Larry was genuinely concerned about my safety and cautioned me not to make any contacts with Bill. The liquor storekeeper agreed with Larry's advice. He added that Bill was so mean even Jones could not do much with him. I told them that I had already made an appointment with him. The liquor storekeeper spewed, "Wha' th' hell's 'n appointment with a logger." Larry's pseudo-cosmopolitan yet unconventional view drastically changed when he began talking about the blacks:

I don't think I'm racist. If I hadn't been in the outside world, I might be a good candidate for it. But, you see, I even married a foreigner . . . see. That's fine. But no matter how much I have changed in my views on races through my experiences in foreign countries, I don't think they [blacks] are the same as the others. You know what I mean? Of course, some of 'em are as good as the white folks. But, most of 'em are somethin' else. You see.

His views about blacks were definite. Again, the liquor storekeeper concurred with Larry.

After a long and tiring day, I was somewhat encouraged, despite Jones's cold reception, to know that if I could develop a good rapport with the whites then I could at least get them to speak out about blacks. Also, I learned that liquor storekeepers could serve as some of the best informants for the project.[16] They knew almost all of the workers. Yet, the responses of the blacks in the community toward me remained to be seen.

Disregarding the warnings, I drove to Harmontown again the next day to meet Bill. I did not stop by Larry's home, although it was located near the road, because I thought he would try to stop me.

Bill's house was located in the middle of nowhere, that is, well off the road in a cotton field. When I arrived, he was not there. However, he had not forgotten the appointment. He had instructed his wife, Ann, to provide any needed information. Since her husband told her to expect my visit, she was not suspicious. I was invited inside. There was only one room which served as the living room, dining room, and bedroom. I saw several *Playboy* magazines. I knew that Bill supposedly could not read or write but figured he must enjoy seeing the pictures. However, I was not sure about Bill's illiteracy. If he was illiterate, then how could he drive the truck? Obtaining a driver's license required a written examination. Incidentally, when I later asked Bill about this while we were talking in the woodyard, he just answered with a big smile. Even now, this remains a mystery to me.

When I asked Ann about Bill's character, she answered, "I never seen Bill's paycheck ever since he been workin' in loggin'." She did not know Bill's wage or his work hours either. She told me her own life history, including a picture of plantation life, sharecropping, and the fun of picking cotton. Also, she clearly indicated the close relationship between Bill's family and the Joneses. Bill was the descendant of a slave for the Jones family. Ann had come to Harmontown from South Carolina when Max and Bob Jones's mother married into the Jones family. Later, the Jones family arranged the marriage between Bill and Ann. According to Ann, Jones had been the major source of their livelihood ever since.

The system of sharecropping was officially gone in this part of the South, but for Bill and Ann matters had changed little, if at all. They had been living in the same wooden shack since marrying, but it had been moved several times whenever the Jones's land holdings were reduced. (The house was on the ground, but it was mobile.) Ann said that the location of her house was the landmark of Jones's land. She became nostalgic when she was talking about the misfortune of the Jones family. For Ann, leaving the employ of the Jones family was unthinkable. The drastic change in the pattern of the landowner's life, from cotton farming to the pulpwood harvesting, brought about a comparable change in this black family's life-style. Their subsistence pattern shifted from farmhand to woodcutter.

When I asked her to comment about the Jones brothers, she avoided making any direct references to the employers of her husband. Yet, she admitted that their grandparents and parents were very generous to the blacks, even though the blacks were worked as slaves. Thus they won the hearts of the blacks. But the Jones brothers were coarse, not only toward the blacks but toward their white neighbors as well. Nevertheless, she worried about them because she did not know what would come next for her and Bill when woodcutting ran out.

Although I enjoyed talking with Ann very much, I had to leave. It was time for her to prepare a meal, and I needed to use a restroom, which they obviously did not have inside their home. Theirs was the cottonfield. I did not wish to "commune with nature" in the open cottonfield. However, I was pleased to have witnessed the friendliness of Ann and her polite manner. My earlier apprehensions about the black family, further exaggerated by the whites in the community, turned out to be imaginary fears.

My preliminary survey of the pulpwood workers had ranged throughout the Piedmont and Coastal Plain in Georgia by mid-April. The extent of pulpwood harvesting activities generally varied according to elevation. In the Piedmont, the pulpwood industry was virtually an outgrowth of the agricultural off-season. Most employees worked only part-time during the off-season. The labor force fluctuated yearly between farming and wood-harvesting.[17] However, on the Coastal Plain, it was an important major industry with full-time workers and year-round production. Also, there were all black crews, all white crews, and mixed crews as well. I concluded that I should plan to do my intensive field work in a community on the Coastal Plain. Thus I began a concentrated search in the Coastal Plain communities.

One day I stopped in Pinetown, Georgia. While I was waiting for the receptionist at the Colonial Motel office, more than ten longwood[18] trucks passed by the motel.[19] A pretty receptionist came in and greeted me with a big smile. Being tired of driving, I was anxious to rest and relax. Before I registered, she asked me if I were an associate of Yamamoto. According to her, Yamamoto and his wife were Japanese-Americans who worked as "chicken sexers." Apparently, because of my features, she thought I was a chicken sexer. They discerned the gender of chickens after incubation. Since poultry was a thriving business in that area of Georgia, they traveled throughout most of the Coastal Plain communities. (Georgia is known for its three P's—poultry, peaches, and pulpwood.) I told her that I came from the university to look around the woodyards and learn about the pulpwood workers in Pinetown. Soon a middle-aged lady, Kathy Hudson, who owned the motel, came in and joined our conversation. She commented that I must be a foreigner from somewhere in the Orient. The receptionist was amazed that her boss had guessed right because she did not think that I could be different from Yamamoto. Kathy explained that she had noticed the difference between our accents. The receptionist began to address me more slowly and clearly. She now knew that she was talking with a foreigner. It seemed to me that my inept English might help me to get their assistance. It might well be an advantage rather than a disadvantage.

I realized that I should go ahead and register, so that I could assure them of my identification. This might eliminate unnecessary suspicions. Kathy was glad to know that I came from the University of Georgia. She had lived in Athens while a student's wife and a business major herself. As a matter of fact, Kathy was a CPA in Pinetown. Her husband, Tom Hudson, had studied forestry. Since I did not know anybody in Pinetown, I decided to utilize Georgia alumni to the utmost.

When Kathy asked me about my job, I told her that I was helping my professor in the study of the pulpwood workers. I asked her if any Georgia alumni had occupations related to the pulpwood industry. Besides her husband, who had been a company forester in the region for the past fifteen years or so, she mentioned Bob Williams, who she felt could be very helpful to my project. He had his own pulpwood crews and was one of three dealers in Pinetown.

Kathy complained about my professor saying, "How in the world could your professor send you, a foreigner, into the woods to study the pulpwood workers? It would be very difficult even for native American students." She obviously did not understand about anthropology.

She tried to figure out how to help me. She asked me how long I planned to stay in town. I answered that if I did my field work there it would take more than three months at least. "Oh Lord!" she said. She placed a call to her husband, but he was not in his office. She promised me to arrange a meeting with her husband. Meantime, I decided to look around the woodyards. When I asked her the directions to the woodyards, she drew a detailed map for me indicating where the woodyards in Pinetown and its vicinity were located. She did not want me to go the woodyards alone. To her, I was a poor, helpless foreigner. She worried about my every move in her town. I was pleased to know that at least I had one sympathizer and a few University of Georgia alumni in the town.

When I drove around the town, I realized that the size of Pinetown was small enough to make it feasible for collecting data on the total community structure if I chose to carry on my intensive study in this community. It had a population of about 4,000 in 1970. My brief tour of the three woodyards impressed me because there were enough crews for comparison on the basis of variety of equipment and types of operation. Upon a suggestion made by Kathy not to make direct contact with the woodyard and also to develop a good rapport with the personnel in the woodyards, I did not walk in the woodyards.

After I returned from a tour of the town, I went by the motel office to carry on further conversation with the receptionist. However, she was already gone and an old lady was substituting for her. She was Kathy's mother. As I introduced myself to her, she told me that she already knew about me. I assumed they had talked about me as soon as I had left the office. I asked her whether she knew Bob Williams. She described him as a "fine young man." According to her, Williams was well known in the town and had made his fortune as a wood dealer. He was one of the hard-working, hard-pushing, energetic, ambitious men in the town. Although he did not participate in any civic group activities or local politics, he was one who could exercise political power whenever necessary. She volunteered, "If you'd like to know about Bob's income and his crews, you ought to talk to Kathy because Kathy helps Bob and other dealers file tax forms every year." I had almost forgotten that Kathy was a CPA in Pinetown. Eventually, her information would be valuable, but I did not think it proper for me to ask another professional to reveal information about her client's personal affairs. I simply told her that I did not want to bother her daughter too much. The old lady did not think it would bother her daughter. She rather liked to demonstrate the important position of her daughter in Pinetown. I knew that Kathy would, indeed, be very helpful for the project, not only as a motel owner and as a wife of a forester, but also as the town's CPA.

I hesitated about whether I should call Bob Williams and make an appointment. I could not help wondering if he might be like the Jones brothers in Harmontown and feared my contact would be unproductive. Bailey might be better for the initial contact, and so I finally concluded that I had better not meet Williams by myself. Bailey could explain matters better than I could, if he agreed that Pinetown was a suitable community for the intensive field work. In that event, Williams would be a key person in assisting the project. If he would willingly help the project, my job in Pinetown would be much easier.[20] Pinetown would be ideal for carrying out the nature of the proposed field work, but only if the leaders of the town would be receptive.[21] Their approval needed to be obtained. I knew that I would need to identify in some ways with the white leadership structure of the community.

I reported my Pinetown findings to Bailey. He was excited about them. And as expected, he wanted to see the community himself and be sure. Before I returned with Bailey to Pinetown, we traveled through a wide range of communities in the Coastal Plain in order to make the best possible decision. As we came into Pinetown, he expressed his agreement with me. He noticed that trucks loaded with harvested wood or pulpwood equipment were common sights. He was pleased to know there were enough crews and workers to study. Three major woodyards, 30 producers, and 165 workers would permit a comparison of equipment, composition, and types of operation.

On this trip to Pinetown, the motel receptionist was again very glad to see me, but she was not quite so enthusiastic about helping me this time. When I had come alone, virtually everybody wanted to help me. As I came down with Bailey, they suddenly became more passive. They did not think I needed so much assistance because I was escorted by an American professor who was supposed to know his own society. For instance, when Bailey asked about a specific locality, they simply told him how to get there without any detailed instructions or map. I speculated that they held the notion that a foreigner might not know anything about American society, so they felt obliged to help him out as much as they could. However, for Bailey, they did not feel they should provide the same assistance. In the shadow of Bailey, I could no longer take advantage of being a foreigner.

Bailey also noted that a lengthy stay by him in Pinetown might not help me. His role appeared to be clear cut. He should introduce me to Williams and read his responses to the project in general and to me in particular. Bailey and I were relieved when we saw Williams's office. It was decorated with Georgia football pennants. We sensed that his strong loyalty to the university from which he graduated assured us of a less-than-cold reception. As we had anticipated, he was very unconventional. Even before Bailey could finish explaining the full details of the project, he declared the necessity of our study. He firmly believed and agreed with us that the problems in pulpwood harvesting were not in technological or mechanical knowledge but were human related.

Bailey asked Williams frankly whether there would be any difficulty for an Asian in carrying out such a project in a community in the Deep South, and specifically whether an Asian could be accepted by the white leadership structure of Pinetown. Williams gave us assurances and promised to protect me during my stay at Pinetown. "First of all, I'll prepare a Country Club membership for him," he said. "And, I'll tell Neal to arrange a meeting with the town leaders one by one." (Neal Boyd, his assistant, was the secretary of a civic club of Pinetown.) To begin with, he allowed me to interact with his company crews at any time. Further, he called up his accountant and instructed her to give us any information we wanted to have, saying he did not think he had anything to hide.

As soon as the main business had ended, Williams started talking about his experiences in Korea during the war. He asked me whether there would be any possible way to find out about a Korean named Lee who worked for him while he was in charge of a military motor pool in Young Deung Po near Seoul, the capital city of Korea. If he could find the boy Lee, he wanted to invite him to Pinetown. And if Lee desired to live in Pinetown, he would gladly make preparations for him and his family. According to Williams, he had never met any person who was a more diligent worker than that boy. He admitted that he needed some diligent workers for his business. Renewing his relations with a Korean in his home town seemed to delight Williams. He continued to talk with me about Korea and Koreans and seemed to forget Bailey's presence.

As he discussed the matter of diligence, he did not forget to mention something about the black workers. He complained that he provided extra work for his black workers every Saturday, but not many of them were interested in taking it, despite the allurement of overtime pay. He brought us a tally sheet which showed the amount of work and each worker's hours for the past year. He wanted to support his statement with statistical data. While experiencing this episode, I realized that the whites, such as Williams, were seemingly outspoken because, as Bailey had anticipated, they saw me as a foreign student who, being neither white nor black, took a neutral position on racial perspectives. I hoped that the blacks would treat me as the whites did.

After having selected Pinetown for the study, I wandered around the town for the first week to gain basic knowledge about the community. Purposefully, while taking my meals, I rotated from place to place around town. During this first stage, I got an impression that nobody in Pinetown seemed concerned about my presence in the town except black children near the Dairy Queen, which was located on the border line between the white and black sections. While I was eating a quick meal there one day, a lot of black children followed me watching with curiosity. Except for that, I was not treated differently. Many anthropological field workers have revealed that in any alien society suspicion is the most common initial reaction. However, I did not feel it in this early stage, possibly because the people in Pinetown felt no threat from my presence.[22] They probably figured that a humble Asian all alone in their town was harmless enough.

I had not lived in a small town like Pinetown since I left my original hometown in my early boyhood. The size of the town did not bother me, but its lack of scenic beauty did. As I drove around the vicinity of Pinetown to carry out a general survey of the crews and producers of each dealer, I was deeply disappointed to see that there were not many trees surrounding the town. About a quarter of a century ago, a southern sociologist, Howard Odum, highly praised the southern forest saying, "Of forests and trees, there were millions of acres in uncounted primeval hardwoods and pines . . . for commerce in cut cordwood for fuel, for paper pulp . . . tall and graceful longleaf and slash of the coastal Plain."[23] The tall and graceful longleaf and slash pines to which Odum referred could no longer be seen along the major transportation routes. Highly mechanized modern pulpwood harvesting methods had cut and removed them. My concern was not that of an environmentalist or forest conservationist. In fact, I was assigned to study the workers who cut the trees. However, I was not pleased to see the places where they had cut them all, known in local terminology as a "clearcut." I wondered how the natural growth rate of the trees, fast though it is in the Coastal Plain, could possibly keep up with the rate of mechanized tree harvesting.[24] If any one was anxious to see the primeval trees, he had to drive more than thirty or forty miles from the major highways.

The layout of Pinetown was simple. Only the spatial arrangement of Pinetown differed slightly from that of most southern county seat towns in which the major traffic patterns focus on the courthouse square and the surrounding central business district. Everyday activities of people in the county traditionally focus on the courthouse square located in the county seat. Conrad Arensberg has characterized the county seat as a community type in the South:

The distinctive community from the South was and is the county. Dispersed a

day's ride in and out around the county seat, that community assembled planta-
tions, free poor white and Negro from the lean hills and swamps, for the pageantry
and the drama of Saturdays round the courthouse, when the courthouse, the jail,
the registry, and the courthouse square shops and lawyers' row made a physical
center of the farflung community.[25]

In Pinetown, the courthouse is located in a residential area outside the main
business area. It was difficult for a stranger to find.

Pinetown's major commercial establishments are located in the business
section in the center of the town with newer businesses beginning to appear
near the edges of the town along the highways. Major industries, mainly
manufacturing firms, are concentrated along the Georgia Southern and
Florida Railway, which runs through the center of the town in a southwest
to northeast direction. The three woodyards are located outside of the city
limits along the Southern Railway. Little tendency toward suburbanization
could be observed. However, the migration of relatively higher income
families out of the town was noticeable.

Pinetown was busy preparing for its centennial celebration. The local
newspaper and radio often brought the centennial celebration to the attention of Pinetowners. I was unable to pick up the mythical or legendary
history. The town is one of a few southern towns which have no historical
sites.

When I visited the Pinetown historian, who was a retired postmaster,
he proudly showed me his working manuscript without hesitation. (Almost
all southern towns have at least one or two local historians whose major
interest is in a folksy, personal account of the regional folklore.) It was filled
with an uncountable number of names. It looked like the beginning of a
verse of the Old Testament. It began with so-and-so is the son of so-and-so
and ended up the same way. The manuscript did not facilitate the acquisi-
tion of the information I was seeking. He was interested in showing me his
family tree and telling stories of the success of his sons, a lawyer and a major
general in the army. I was impressed by the gigantic pictures of his sons
hanging on the wall. I realized that he seemed to pride himself in displaying
everything he had, while I was eager to know only that relating to the
historic development of Pinetown.

After spending several hours listening to his family story, I was able to
gather a few facts on the industrial development of Pinetown. According to
him, in earlier days, the economy of the town centered around agriculture,

mainly tobacco. Cotton was never a major part of the economy of Pinetown. Pulpwood became important after the construction of paper mills throughout the Coastal Plain in the early twentieth century. Forest-related industries increased in importance until the end of World War II. Soon after that, several large manufacturing companies located plants in Pinetown. In recent years, there has again been considerable growth in the forest-related industries.

Pinetown is governed by a city government, consisting of a mayor and city commissioners elected for two-year terms. The head of the city commission also serves as a city manager. I went to the city hall many times during the first week of my stay to meet the mayor, but I was unable to see him. Later, I learned that the mayor was a physician. He had been busy taking care of his patients. Finally, when I became a patient because of an earache, I had a chance to meet him. According to him, I had contracted the malady in the woods while with the wood workers. He said it was common among them. Incidentally, he had graduated from the University of Georgia and was excited that the university had initiated such a study in his town. I was encouraged by his supportive attitude. I would need his dual assistance as mayor and physician in Pinetown, as did most of the citizens in the town. The nurse in the physician's office was kept busy determining whether each visitor was a patient or someone to see the mayor.

In Pinetown, there are a number of civic clubs. Among them, the Junior Chamber of Commerce and the Rotary Club were the most active ones. Since the nature of my field work was directly related to the understanding of other industries, the Junior Chamber of Commerce was to serve not only as a source of information but also as a mediator. I had frequent contact with the membership of the Rotary Club, which represented a wide variety of occupations and positions in the community.

Although one-fourth of the population was black, no blacks participated as members of the local elite in political office or in any of the civic clubs. This structure of political and civic organizations in Pinetown strongly suggested to me that I should stay in good stead with the white leadership structure and be discreet about my contacts with blacks.

2

Living in Pinetown, Georgia

One evening, a day's wandering in the woods being over, I was voraciously hungry and went to the newly opened Colonial Motel Restaurant for my evening meal. I quickly went through three glasses of iced tea; its sweetness just made me more thirsty. (In most of the southern restaurants, the iced tea is ready-made sweet tea. That will not seem unusual to Americans, but Orientals fix tea differently.) I ordered a large T-bone steak. As is customary, a salad preceded the regular meal. And as is my custom, I did not touch it despite my appetite. Salads look to me like a vegetable garden come to the table. The waitress indicated wonderment at this stranger who did not touch his salad. During the meal, she returned and inquired as to my choice of dessert; I thanked her and said I did not care for any. With this, she could hardly control her laughter until she got into the kitchen where she shared this new experience with the cook. They laughed loudly enough that I could hear it.

Since I came to America, I have generally handled the resocialization process quite successfully. But I have had great difficulty in adjusting my food habits. I agree with the belief that early learning lasts. I have found it difficult to eat vegetables or sweet treats apart from the main course and do not prefer salads or desserts. While in Pinetown, I usually chose American foods which are similar to Oriental foods, such as mixtures of vegetables and meat. The closest-related item was vegetable soup. I asked for vegetable soup virtually every meal except breakfast. I also found that it was a choice that stood me in good stead with the waitress. Whenever I took a bowl of vegetable soup, the waitress did not ask me about salad or dessert.

One evening a few weeks later, the restaurant was not busy; the

45

waitress, a bus boy, and the cook were sitting in the dining hall. They were exchanging the local gossip. As I came in, the bus boy said, "Here comes the bird." The others laughed. I was curious about what the boy meant. I did not know much about English curse words. I had no way of knowing whether "bird" was an epithet for Orientals or not. Having traveled the gravel forest roads seventy or eighty miles that day, I ordered a large steak instead of the usual vegetable soup. Again, I ate only the meat, and set aside everything else. The same waitress came to me and tried to teach me the proper table manners. It was an ideal opportunity because no other customers were there. "Even though you don't like the salad, you got to pay for it, you know," she advised, "and in the American way, you've got to take dessert after the meal. That's the way it goes." I told her that I did not know much about American ways and would be pleased if she could offer me more advice. She was so pleased by my acceptance that she at once voluntarily explained to me about the reference to a bird. It had not been used in a derogatory way but was related instead to my light eating. She felt sorry about it and could not stop laughing. "See, you eat so little, just like a bird," she said, "That's why. Don't feel bad about it." She laughed again along with the other waitresses. The bus boy disappeared and did not come back while I was staying there.

That episode awakened me to the fact that the Pinetowners were already observing my behavior as seriously as I was theirs. I realized that my activities and behavior in the town had been taken into account thoroughly. I did not know how other anthropologists had felt about such circumstances when the natives made their own participant-observations of the anthropologists; but as for me, my activities and behavior in Pinetown became more cautious. As a result, I found myself becoming more Asian-like, because I felt more secure with these norms which I knew best.

No matter how I interpreted it, I could not feel comfortable about the fact that they were observing me. I thought about moving away from the motel and managing for myself. If I continued to stay in the motel and take meals in the restaurant, there was no way I could hide my activities. If I rented my own place, this would provide a chance to bring my family down. Also, I could cook my own meals and not worry about the salads and desserts. I did not want to be studied by the townspeople. And so I bought a weekly town newspaper and went back to my room at the motel to search the ads for a suitable room or house.

As soon as I got back to my room in the motel, I noticed at once that some of my materials were gone. My preliminary data on the pulpwood crews, their equipment, and the list of the workers' names had disappeared. My field notes were also missing. Virtually all of my materials written in English had disappeared.

Until that incident, I frankly did not realize the necessity of making duplications of every field note and data sheet. Every morning when I had sent off the extra copies to the university at the town post office, I had little known the real value of doing it. I had considered it an unnecessary ritual in anthropological field work. I finally understood why the experienced field workers instruct the beginners to do this.[1] Having sent carbon copies of the now lost material to the university, I could recover it by making a trip to the university. If I had not done as my professor instructed me, I would have lost a month or more of my work in the field. I was not particularly amenable to learning such field methods the hard way.

Although my loss could be salvaged, I felt insecure knowing someone was so interested in my activities in the town, and I began to be concerned about my safety there. That night, I was so immersed in thinking of alternative plans for my stay in Pinetown that I could not sleep.

The fears I had in that motel room were difficult to describe. I was wondering, if anyone wished to interfere with my field work, the means would be well planned and skillfully carried out.

My fears grew as I better comprehended the contents of the stolen material. In my field notes, I had candidly written everything I observed along with personal commentaries which might easily irritate Pinetowners. This included my assessment of racial relations in Pinetown. I had noted that, regardless of the enactment of the 1964 Civil Rights Act, any adjustments to desegregation in private commercial establishments in Pinetown were not readily visible. For instance, except in a place where one could pick up his order quickly, I had never seen blacks in the first-class restaurants in the town. Since I never saw any black attempting to enter those restaurants, I was unable to observe any specific sanctions which might have been used to keep the blacks away from such places. Thus, I could not tell whether desegregation was creating a form of "resegregation" as described when Killian used the term in *White Southerners*.[2] I was surprised to find no form of segregation against a nonwhite Asian. An observation made by Burgess as early as 1928 and cited by Myrdal in 1944 in *An American Dilemma* indicated that "Orientals and possibly Mexicans among all separate ethnic groups have as much segregation as the Negro."[3] This description was not in accordance with my experiences in Pinetown.

I had said in my notes that since Pinetown is so small, the black residential section is not spatially separated from that of the whites. In the town, there is no railroad track which commonly serves as a clear racial boundary between blacks and whites. However, a great social and ceremonial distance between these two sections did exist. It seemed as if two different worlds existed within the same small town. Accordingly, this separation was maintained in every aspect of social life, except in the use of the general store owned by a white. The general store was located on the border line between the white and black sections and stayed open until midnight. The blacks could use it after the other stores had closed. As a matter of fact, this store dominated the economy of the blacks. Although the owner of the general store was cordial to me, I felt sorry for the blacks who patronized the store.

I also had criticized the servile manner by which older black workers addressed their white boss [such as "yes, sir'ee," "you got it," or "sho' nuff"]. I rarely heard any black workers saying "no" to their white boss. Generally, the black workers affirmed and reaffirmed the wishes of the white boss. They revealed a lack of contrariness, aggressiveness, and independent individuality in relating to the whites. On many occasions when there was no way to finish a job in a given time in accordance with the instructions of the white boss, a black worker would continue to say he could do so; and when he did not finish he would simply remain a lazy, disgraceful black worker in the opinion of the white boss. It also seemed to me that a good many blacks spoiled their white bosses. Therefore, if an independent-minded young black did not conform to the established expectations of the whites, he would be classified as a "bad Negro" from the spoiled white man's view. John Dollard's description in 1937 of black behavior toward whites in his *Class and Caste in a Southern Town* still appeared to be accurate for the most part.[4] If there were such a thing as a "systematic and integrated structure" which served to isolate the black and white groups from each other in the South as Myrdal has indicated,[5] it would be difficult for one to blame whites only. The races would be mutually responsible for the manifestation.

One of my lost possessions was a list of welfare recipients who were pulpwood workers. I was afraid of repercussions for those workers if that data became known to the public. Another list named the members of various crews who were paid by cash instead of regular paychecks.

What concerned me most about the loss of my field notes was the loss of descriptions of several individuals and their personal stories. If that portion became public knowledge, then I would be in a very embarrassing position regarding my interviewees, whose confidentiality I had promised to protect.

One such person discussed in my notes was George Moore. Moore was working at the railroad station as a consultant. He never mentioned many details about his job. His job required that he travel from one station to another working only a few months at each. He and I were the only long-term guests at the motel, so eventually we became acquaintances. We often dined together for the evening meal. He always ordered inexpensive meals and left no tip for the waitress. However, he made girl friends easily. One evening he invited me to go out with him and said he had already arranged a girl friend for me. I was embarrassed by the offer. If it became known in the community that I had gone out with a local girl at night, it would jeopardize my field work in Pinetown. In answer, I told him that I was married and had two sons. He seemed astounded at my unwillingness. After I rejected his offer, we were never very close again.[6]

Another person I had discussed was the local newspaper editor. I had met him at a civic club luncheon meeting when I was invited as a guest speaker. He was a member and appeared to be a very handsome and affable young man. After my speech was over, most of the members showed interest in my project. But he neither asked questions nor spoke a friendly word. Nevertheless, I was eager to make his acquaintance since he was the major source of local news. I must admit, however, that throughout my stay in Pinetown he was not hostile toward me. Rather, he simply ignored my presence in the town. He was proud of his unique role as a young intellectual in the town and apparently did not want to admit the existence of a doctoral candidate in Pinetown, although my stay would be temporary.

I once visited his office while conducting a survey of the community leaders' attitudes toward the pulpwood workers and the pulpwood industry as a whole. When I reminded him of our previous encounter, he pretended not to remember me and denied the event of our meeting, although it had been only about ten days before. He refused to answer my questionnaire. He also denied me permission to go through his newspaper file of recent editions to verify information. He declared that his newspapers were not filed to serve such a purpose. I left my questionnaire with him and went away. He returned it almost immediately without filling out any information. Not only did he ignore me but my work as well in his newspaper, which usually reported everything in the community. My anthropology textbooks and lectures had not addressed the problem of handling hard-liners or discussed ways to approach such lay-intellectuals and develop them into good respondents. In this case, I could only give up.

I decided to do nothing about the loss of my data and field notes. Since there was very little hope of recovering the materials, I did not mention the incident to the motel owner. If I had done so, rumors would inevitably have spread around the town. I preferred to behave as though nothing had happened. I would take my own security measures in the future to protect my data.[7] First of all, I had to determine whether I should remain in the motel or move elsewhere. I could rent a house and have more privacy. As far as personal safety was concerned, however, the motel would be a little better. And if I moved I would lose the motel restaurant waitress and motel receptionist as my key informants about town activities. My final decision was to remain in the motel. Thus, I had to figure a strategy for the security of my data. I decided to write everything in Korean. I would send off the previous day's data collection to the university early in the morning. To secure incoming mail, I obtained my own post office box and ceased receiving mail at the motel office.

That night I waited impatiently for morning instead of falling asleep. Finally, I decided I should at least report my presence in Pinetown to the office of county sheriff the next morning. Although I had resolved to say nothing of my loss, I would feel better knowing that he knew of my activities. As I hurried to my car after breakfast, I found a note stuck in the windshield wiper of my car. It was written on the inside of a cigarette package. The short message said, "If you don't want to be hurt, keep away from the loggers." Interestingly enough, since I had slept lightly the night before, I should have heard anyone who approached my car because it was parked right beside my room. It was a strange feeling for a lone anthropologist to find a threat in an alien town. Obviously, someone was attempting to chase me away. Everything had gone smoothly for a month or more, and everything had suddenly gone wrong two days in a row.

My next move was to go to the office of the sheriff. The officer wore plain clothes, making it difficult for me to tell whether he was the sheriff or the deputy. But before I could tell him my name, he greeted me by name. He had already found out about me. I told him I was a graduate student in anthropology at the university studying Pinetown and its relation to the pulpwood workers. He asked me sincerely, "What's anthropology, by the way?" Someone sitting in the office answered quickly, "That's the study of primitive people." I was rather surprised to know that somebody knew something about anthropology even if it was only partially true. "D'you mean to say that we're primitive people?" the officer inquired sullenly. I attempted to explain that anthropology studies modern man as well. However, it was too late to change his view of anthropology. "Have you met enough primitives in Pinetown?" he persisted sneeringly. It seemed that everything was going wrong. Maybe I should have said I was a graduate student in sociology. Our department was then a joint department of sociology and anthropology.

Abandoning the fruitless explanation, I decided to ask him about the crime rate of the pulpwood workers in Pinetown. By then, I had already collected considerable information about the jail experiences of the pulpwood workers. A good number of pulpwood workers had been in jail several times, but usually only for minor charges related to fighting and drunkenness. A common practice was that a producer would bail out his jailed worker in order to put him back to work. Nevertheless, the officer's answer was a ready-made one: "They are as good a citizens as you are. As a matter of fact, I don't have any problem with them," he said. "How about David Wright?" I countered, referring to one worker who had been jailed at least four times recently. "You ask David," he said sharply, "He'd tell you better." I stood up and walked out of his office. For his part, he did not even look my way. I knew that it was unwise to show my temper while in the field, particularly with a local official. But I could not help it that very moment, and I regretted having visited him on that already frustrating day.

Later that day, after arranging for a post office box, I went to the office of a dealer, Tony Tyler, who had the largest number of producers in the region. He was involved in so many community activities that I had never had a chance to meet him until then. And since I had an appointment, I could not very well postpone the meeting. I did not expect a very productive discussion because such a well-arranged meeting seldom produced remarkable results. He was polite but very formal. He asked me, "I reckon you are studying at the university, are you not?" I answered that I was, without suffixing "sir." I was anticipating that the next question would be about my discipline and forgot to say "yes, sir." I sensed immediately that he was displeased with my manner of answering.[8] Again, I was wondering if I should say my discipline was sociology in order to skip the issue of "primitives." However, his next question differed from my expectations. He wanted to know how a person from an "underdeveloped country" could conduct an investigation of the most advanced society. He strongly resented my role as a researcher in his community. I did not know what I should do. At least, I should avoid the mistake which I had made in the sheriff's office. I concluded that I should play the part of the Asian stereotype: be humble, polite, and appreciative. I told him that I was not the principal investigator for the project. My professor was conducting the project and I was just an assistant helping with the project. I added that I was taking this opportunity to learn American culture, particularly southern culture, in depth. I explained that although many foreign students have studied in America, few of them had such a rare chance to study real American life in such depth, because they remained on their college campuses almost exclusively. I told him that I would like very much his allowing me to observe the mechanized harvesting methods and sophisticated machinery of his producers' crews. I emphasized that my observing and talking with the workers in a natural setting would be more valuable than learning in a classroom or library. He agreed with my view and changed his mood. I told him that, being a foreigner, I could not adequately express my way of thinking in English. Furthermore, I told him I did not know southern customs since I was in the process of learning American ways. "Don't worry about it," he said kindly, "I'll fix everythin' I can for you."

Tyler called in Bobby Rodgers, one of his procurers (one who buys and looks after timberlands for a dealer) and instructed him to assist me in every way. When I asked for specific data on pulpwood harvesting, Tyler not only complied but also phoned the agriculture extension agent insisting that he accommodate my inquiries. He behaved as if he were my host in Pinetown. I could not have expected better treatment from anyone. He even asked me whether my stay in town was comfortable or not. I learned from this relationship why some blacks would "Uncle Tom" the whites.

I asked Rodgers to arrange a meeting between me and Ed Smith, a black producer and worker. His was a marginal crew composed of himself only. He had the longest work experience of any worker in the region. He was a native Pinetowner who had had seven years of formal education. He was hauling his wood to Williams's woodyard when I had first contacted him to make an overall survey of the producers and equipment in Pinetown and its vicinity. While I was contacting each producer in Williams's woodyard, he suddenly quit and switched to Tyler's woodyard in order to avoid my contact. Rodgers said that he might help make such an arrangement. Rodgers had been a rural mail carrier for the last fifteen years, so he knew almost everyone. He was known as a nice person among the blacks.

Smith was an important person for my study because he represented the traditional way of pulpwood harvesting. He was unique; the only one-man crew remaining. He was enrolled in the welfare assistance program but had two other jobs as part-time custodian in a local bank and part-time pulpwood producer. His production and working schedule varied every week. This made it difficult to meet with him. Whenever I talked to other pulpwood workers, particularly whites, they were very critical about the welfare program of the government as a whole and were very hostile toward Smith in particular. This occurred because he was a welfare recipient while retaining his additional sources of income.

On that very day with the assistance of Rodgers, I found Smith in the general store located near the black section. I explained my purpose in Pinetown. Rodgers gave his assurance that I came from the university rather than from the government or a paper company. By request, I showed my student identification card, but still Smith remained suspicious. My efforts and the assistance of Rodgers did not produce any positive results at all. Smith remained deceptive and vague so that I could not gain access to his genuine perceptions.

When I finally returned to my motel room, I was exhausted from the events of the day. I did not feel like eating anything, even vegetable soup. I was very frustrated and threw myself on my bed. Suddenly, the motel receptionist called me and said, "Hey, the Yamamoto couple are here. They're waitin' for you at the restaurant." Although I had never met them before, I was anxious to meet them. Frankly, I still had some special feelings about Japanese owing to the antagonisms that developed while the Japanese occupied Korea during most of my boyhood. However, when the motel receptionist called me, I did not remember those old enmities at all. I was happy to know that they were in Pinetown. I cannot give any adequate explanation of why, unless I figured we shared many of the same feelings because we were fellow Asians in an alien society. I rushed to the restaurant at once. I had no trouble recognizing Yamamoto and his wife, and they had no difficulty recognizing me either. They appeared to be as happy as I about our meeting. I enjoyed eating my meal for the first time since I had come to Pinetown.

I related to them my day's experiences which still preoccupied my mind. I was particularly intrigued by the unusual generosity of Tyler after my stereotyped Oriental behavior. Yamamoto said he was glad I had found that out. As long as I maintained my Oriental accent and behaved as an Oriental, he felt I would be all right in the South. California, where he had been born and raised, was different, he said, because there are so many Orientals around.[9]

He told me his observations of southerners:

Most of the southerners are friendly when they see my name or face knowing I'm a helpless foreigner. But, as soon as I start to speak English, they suddenly treat me differently. You see, I don't know anything about Japan. You probably know more than I do. I really don't know the manner of Orientals. My grandparents were born in Japan and came to America. That's all I know about. Usually people say, "Hey, you speak English just like us." Don't try to be equal with these people. If you can demonstrate superiority over them with visible evidence, then go ahead. If they can admit it, they really will respect you. But, this would be very difficult for us to do though.

His polite and quiet wife added, "Karate men are a good example of this. They surely show their superior abilities with clear evidence." Her husband nodded and continued, "As to my job as chicken sexer, if I was not accurate about 95 percent or higher all the time, they wouldn't invite me to Pinetown and all these other towns every month. They respect my accuracy at least. Don't compete with 'em. If you do, then they'll pick on you and step on you. The best thing for you to do is be a foreigner admitting that you don't know anything about American culture. You can do that, but I cannot."

"What about the blacks?" I asked him, having had so much trouble conversing with Smith. "I've had very little chance to be around them," Yamamoto said. "But I do know one thing. They don't care much about other minorities—no sympathy whatsoever."[10] His wife added, "They don't like Orientals because most of the Orientals are doing better than the average blacks, I think." She carefully waited for the response of her husband. "I guess none of the minority groups want to remain at the bottom," he commented.

They planned to work like machines all night discerning the gender of chickens. They were paid one cent per chicken. If the couple worked all night without taking any breaks, they could make five hundred dollars.

Before we left the restaurant, Yamamoto asked me if I had any children. I told him I had two sons. He sighed and paused for a while without saying anything. Then he said with quiet sincerity, "You better go back to your homeland as soon as you finish your study no matter what your status will be after you get back home. I don't want to see any second or third generation Orientals go through what I have gone through."

Yamamoto promised me that the next month when he came to Pinetown he would tell me about his life in a Japanese relocation camp. He was one of those West Coast Japanese who were maintained in such a camp during World War II (after the spring of 1942). He firmly believed that Japanese relocation was a case of racism.[11] That concluded an unusually active day of my living in Pinetown. Because of the upbeat day and lack of sleep the previous night, nothing could have prevented my sleep that night.

Despite such frustrating experiences, my routine observation about the pulpwood crews continued daily. According to my observation, in the Pinetown region, many pulpwood crews were racially mixed. The mixed crew existed only under white producerships. While a good many blacks worked for the white producers, no white workers were employed by the black producers.

Since Al Swain was a black producer, all his workers were blacks. Although his crew was known as one of the most efficient crews in the region and was paid higher wages than others, no white workers had ever asked to work for him. Because of our frequent contact, the workers in Swain's crew became acquainted with me and would occasionally tease me. Once they pushed my car into the woods for fun. I had to wait until they helped me get it out. I was pleased by their friendliness. However, sometimes their practical jokes were so deliberate that it was hard for me to understand they were only teasing.

I remember the occasion on which they had a good time killing a rattlesnake. As soon as I came on the scene, one worker threw the snake at me. I screamed and ran because I did not know whether it was dead or not.

They laughed and laughed at me. It must have been the most fun they had ever had in the woods. Frankly, I was not happy about it, even though it was an indication that I had developed good rapport with the workers. Somehow I managed to calm myself down. Bobby Rodgers who accompanied me was surprised when I said nothing about the incident to either Swain or the worker. Swain was so embarrassed about it that he did not know what he should do.

As usual I waited around until Swain was available for answering a few questions. When he was available, he suggested that we would find a better time and place where we could talk more. He felt bad because I usually waited many hours sometimes, meanwhile enduring severe chiding from his men, only to receive brief answers to my questions. As a result, he invited me to have dinner in his home on a weekend. I readily accepted. In fact, I had been waiting for such an invitation from a black.

I followed Rodgers to see the selective cutting of Tony Tyler's tree farm for the rest of the afternoon. During our several months' association, we had become good friends. We talked about almost everything with little reservation. For instance, he asked me about choices of colleges and a major area of study for his son. I tried to give my best advice. During afternoon breaks, I lay down beside Rodgers under the shadow of a tree to cool off a little. Rodgers broke the silence and said, "I reckon you've got a sense of pride or somethin'. But I can't understan' how you can be so patient. I've seen it twice at least. When you were talkin' to Tyler a couple of months ago in our office, you remember? I heard most o' the talk. You were so polite. If I were you, I couldn't stand for it. I can't believe you Orientals can do it. Again, today, when that colored guy threw the rattlesnake atcha [at you], you didn't say nothin' to 'im. Don't you gotta temper?"

Instead of praising my manner of reacting, Rodgers was wondering about me. Although he phrased his question in a modified form, what he was asking was: "Are you human like me?" Basically, he felt I was being too servile and unnecessarily humble. Of course, as that was not my true nature, I wished to give a witty reply such as "I did not sell out my soul but have just rented it during my field work." But I could not afford to become that familiar with Rodgers while he was still my field informant. I had to remember I was talking with a native in the field. I did not know how much I should expose myself to a native. My training in anthropology had not alluded to this feature of an ethical challenge. Should an anthropologist maintain dual personalities in the field, not always telling the truth to the native people? In this case, I answered him jokingly, "Because of that, I met a good friend like you and got an invitation to eat a free meal at Swain's house." He was unsatisfied with my reply but did not seem to suspect that I was hiding my true emotions.

Swain's invitation pleased me very much. Although I had visited several black families previously, it was my first formal dinner invitation. His house was not located in the black section of town. It was about eight miles away from the city limits of Pinetown. I envisaged a small rundown shanty in which a large extended family shares only one or two beds in the same room.[12] His house would undoubtedly be poorly constructed, unpainted, in need of repairs, and without indoor toilet facilities and hot running water. This presupposition was engendered by my previous visits in black homes.[13] The unpaved dirt road I turned down confirmed my expectations. At the end of a slow curve in the dirt road, there was indeed a small, unprepossessing, weatherbeaten cottage with peeling paint. There was no neighbor for more than a mile.

But as Swain led me into his house, my assumptions turned out to be unfounded. The room was paneled with pine wood, and clean rugs were on the floor. Every piece of furniture was nice and clean. Several picture frames hung on the wall. It was absolutely unbelievable considering the exterior of the house. And instead of being crowded, the couple lived alone, having only a married son who no longer lived with them. I felt guilty about my assumptions.

I was surprised when told that I was their first guest, white or black, to come inside the house since they had remodeled its interior. That certainly aroused my interest so I asked them how that could be. "Well, y' know, white folks won't come in," Swain said. "If they want me, they stop by outside 'n holler 'n I come out." "If they'd come inside of ar' house, yo' know, they wouldn't like it," his wife commented. They had intentionally left the outside in its dilapidated condition.

I then asked them why blacks had not visited them. The couple looked at each other and hesitated. They appeared reluctant to disparage other blacks to a nonblack. "It's a shame for me, a black, to talk about other blacks this way," Swain said, "But it's true though. If my men were inside of my house one evening, they'd line up the next day askin' me for loans. I couldn't afford to do it. If I wanna keep my men, I can't give 'em loans. If I do, I'll never see 'em again."

I was already familiar with the practice of loans between producer and worker. It had long been a deep-rooted problem, having originated in the structure of the pulpwood industry itself. Because almost all of the workers found it impossible to repay loans, they simply repaid them by selling their labor. This caused a pattern of high labor turnover. Theoretically, the relationship between a worker and his producer should be that of employer and employee. In practice, the industry has been maintained by a paternal relationship similar to that between slaveowners and slaves. The producer is expected to take care of his workers and their families in exchange for labor. For instance, when a worker is arrested by the local police or entangled in the judicial process, the producer posts bail for his worker. And when a worker wants money, usually he can successfully obtain a loan from his producer, even in nonemergency situations. If a request is rejected, the worker frequently looks for another producer who will give him the loan.

Swain discussed specifically the loan-related problems of Richard Horn, a white producer. He had opened his house to his workers but eventually found he could not afford the practice. His workers thought he was very rich. Horn had already talked to me about his problem. He had tried to help his workers out by giving them his own money, but that had turned out to be disastrous. Abandoning that means, he was trying to help them in some other way. When he received a request for a loan, he took the worker to the local bank and helped him get the loan. He said that method was very successful and resulted in positive contributions for his workers and him-self. He could keep his workers when he helped them to get the loan. The workers felt better psychologically about repaying the bank rather than him. Most importantly, the bank records helped the workers in establish-ing credit in the community.

After the dinner of country ham and baked potatoes, Swain and I continued to discuss the pulpwood workers. He complained that his workers claimed he made more money than he actually did. The real difference, he insisted, was simply that he managed his money much better than they. For instance, since all equipment was furnished, they had no job-related expenses. Yet, problems arose because they spent their money as though every day was payday, he said. And very often they spent more than they earned. Interestingly enough, their wages were actually higher than those of local factory workers.

Then he mentioned some specific problems of Horn, who was known to be the most efficient producer in the region. He asked me if Horn's operation did not look very impressive. I admitted that it did. Horn's crew harvested longwood, which required much heavy, sophisticated equipment. He said that:

Horn's got more problems than I've got. He's invested huge sums o' money for that machinery. If he hadn't, he couldn't stay in the longwood business n' he couldn't get no worker to work for 'im, yo' know. The youngsters now days like t' work wi' machines. They don't like hard work. Yo' know wha' I mean? For that, he owes more money to the bank than anyone else around here. I doubt that he can make any money out of it.

Horn had not exposed this problem to me. He had always demonstrated to me that he was one of the most efficient producers and a very capable businessman.

Swain also felt that Horn spoiled his crew too much. He could not see how an individual producer could afford to set up a benefit system like those offered by the factories and readily admitted he could not do it. Swain hinted that most of the young pulpwood workers were interested in getting jobs in manufacturing plants because they realized the importance of a benefit system for their future. This conversation motivated me to survey the manufacturing workers in town.

Before I left Swain's home, I asked him why he had invited me into his home while avoiding such amenities with trusted blacks and whites. Again he emphasized that he had felt bad because he was so busy in the woods that I had to wait hours for him and, even then, his answers had to be short. He and his wife had discussed it. They had decided to invite me so that we might talk longer and more comfortably.

I then asked a follow-up question about whether they would have extended the same invitation had I been either a white or black researcher. His wife smiled without saying anything. Swain grinned and said, "I don' believe so, I sure don'." Reading the response of his wife, he continued, "If you were a white, I don't think you'd come in my house for a meal. And if you were a black, frankly I'd be more cautious about invitin' you to my place. You're a foreigner. I figure you don' care for local gossip or anythin'

like that. And I don' have to worry about yo' to puttin' on airs about us." As
I nodded, he and his wife smiled.

I also asked his help in persuading Ed Smith, a black producer whom I
have mentioned previously, to cooperate with my study. Swain seemed very
reluctant to associate with other blacks in the region. But he replied that
Smith had told him about me. Smith had thought I was a government
agent. Some whites in the woodyard had teased Smith telling him that I had
come to investigate him about his welfare checks. Swain assured me that he
would explain to Smith that I came from the university to study the workers
and not as a government agent. That evening was one of the most pleasant I
spent in Pinetown. The Swains were hospitable, considerate, and very
informative.

In the latter part of my field work, I had to compile comparative data on
the life patterns of the pulpwood workers and the manufacturing plant
workers. But before I could do this, I had to conduct a socioeconomic survey
of the manufacturing workers, using the same guidelines as in a similar
survey of the pulpwood workers. There were only four manufacturing firms
in Pinetown so I thought the survey would not take too long. That
assumption weakened significantly when I learned to my chagrin that the
four plants employed 2,147 workers.

Considering that the population of the town was only 4,065 and the
outlying area sparsely populated, the plants employed a large majority of
the Pinetown area work force. For the first time, I realized the tremendous
impact of northern manufacturing industries on small southern towns.
Although the production of raw materials in Pine County, e.g., 5 million
pounds of tobacco, and 100,000 cords of pulpwood in 1970, was impressive, the growing number of wage earners employed by manufacturing
plants in the town could not be underestimated. This source of employment
was undoubtedly the single most important trend in the life and economy of
Pinetown. As a matter of fact, many community leaders had manifested
that idea to me during my survey of their attitudes toward the pulpwood
industry. However, at the time, I had been ignorant of the number of
factory workers and had not understood. Also, as a relative newcomer to the
South, I had not been aware of the trend or of the resulting dramatic
changes.

Nearly forty years ago, Howard Odum, proclaimed that the South had a "colonial economy." His notion was derived from the fact that the southern region served as a supplier of raw material to other regions, which in turn was processed and shipped back as finished products.[14] However, after World War II, Odum's description no longer applied. As American industries were booming with the reconstruction of Europe, they began to look for areas with cheap yet reliable nonunion labor. In the South, they not only found cheap, dependable labor but also cheap electric power. Thus the basic economic structure of southern towns shifted drastically during the postwar years. Soon many southern towns were leaning more toward an industrial orientation than their traditionally agricultural one. Pinetown was no exception.

Southern political leaders had eagerly supported the North's economic interests even before the war. The Mississippi legislature enacted a law in the mid-1930s permitting cities to finance through referendums the construction of new buildings to lure industries and allowing five-year tax exemptions.[15] The similar plan adopted in Georgia varied only slightly. The basic plan was the same throughout most of the southern states.

In speaking to the legislature about passage of the original bill, Governor Hugh White of Mississippi said, "Our high percentage of native Anglo-Saxon citizenship, with an absence of the disturbing elements so common to large industrial centers, offers a great attraction for those looking for new fields in which to establish their factories."[16] This served as an open invitation to employers in all regions of the country. Both southerners and the northern-based employers realized the invitation as an offer of cheap labor with no labor unions attached.

There was some resistance to this trend, particularly by southern intellectuals. The book called *I'll Take My Stand,* published in 1930 by a dozen agrarians from Vanderbilt University, is a good summary of this concern.[17] They phrased their warnings about the effects of industrialization on the southern region. Their warnings were well reflected in the dramatic writing of Louis Rubin:

All around them the young Southern writers saw a country doing its best to become "modern," "progressive," "up-to-date," and as they viewed it, achieving only faddishness, unbelief, and a tawdry commercialism. In the South's eager race to emulate the rest of the country, all the things that they had been taught were good were being cast aside. Business was in the saddle; the chamber of commerce reigned.[18]

With the aid of the local Junior Chamber of Commerce, my visits to Pinetown's manufacturing plants were easily arranged. I had already met most of the executives at local civic club meetings. All of them were northerners who were born, reared, and educated in the North, because their home firms were located in the North. Killian accurately assessed such industries in the South when he said, "Often the best-paid employees, the executives and the skilled workers, were imported from other parts of the nation."[19] The executives in Pinetown's manufacturing firms proudly showed me their facilities and products. When we approached the major business, they became very formal. After glancing over my prepared interview schedule for their workers, each refused to allow me to administer my questionnaires. They said that it would disturb their work plan. But it became apparent that they did not like certain items on the questionnaire, such as questions related to wages and attitudes toward labor unions. One of the executives whose plant employed more than a thousand workers told me that his workers did not see a necessity for one since they were paid enough and treated well. In fact, none of the manufacturing plants in Pinetown had a labor union.

One of the executives privately admitted that Pinetown offered certain advantages to prospective manufacturing firms while he was explaining the history of his plant in Pinetown. Cheaper wages coupled with freedom from labor disputes had made Pinetown very attractive to his firm. Such firms looked upon the poverty-stricken rural whites and blacks primarily as a source of cheap, tractable labor.[20] Although this trend became established after World War II in Pinetown, it was a continuation of the earlier movement toward industrialization that had begun in the 1930s in other parts of the South.

My conversations with the executives constituted my first formal contacts with northerners living in the South. The "transplanted Yankees" as Killian referred to them differed greatly from the "southern gentleman" mold.[21] They were extremely formal and constantly remained in their roles of businessmen. They extended no special treatment to a foreigner. Even if I behaved as an alien, there was no sympathy or special considerations. One might say the southerners had spoiled me with their politeness and special treatment. No matter what one might call it, I surely missed the southern hospitality when in the company of the northern executives.

My amazement came not in regard to their cool and undifferentiated treatment of a foreign researcher but rather to their language usage. I was shocked to hear the transplanted Yankee executives referring to blacks as "colored men." Until then, I had entertained optimistic expectations, thinking the northerners might possibly provide a leavening influence on southern racial attitudes. I had considered it not unrealistic to expect people not raised in the racial order of the South to introduce an element of heterodoxy that would eventually bring about changing attitudes in the South. Killian has given a good explanation of why they should not be expected to bring about such changes:

> The most unlikely reason is that they desire to reform the natives of the host community. Ministers and college professors (and civil rights activists) may sometimes move to the South as missionaries, but businessmen and manufacturers do not. Their motives are economic. These motives have included new markets, tax abatements, sources of raw materials, and avoidance of union-management conflicts. One of the things the Yankee manager of a southern plant least wants is to get into a fight with the local population over race relations.[22]

Indeed, they had thoroughly conformed to the norms of the southern communities. They tried to maintain good community relations. They joined the chamber of commerce, affiliated with the church of their choice, and sought membership in the civic clubs. As Killian has described, "In doing so, he [the transplanted Yankee manager] exposes himself to the conservative end of the spectrum of White southern opinion, and he is not likely to challenge rudely the pronouncements of his new associates on the way we have handled the race problem down here."[23] The belief held by the transplanted Yankee managers was that "we are not the crusaders."[24]

Actually, in the South, a paradoxical situation exists. The economic structure which is commonly cited as discriminatory to blacks discriminates against whites as well. Both blacks and poor whites have certainly endured job discrimination. But there is yet another form of ever present discrimination in the South. The new economic structure which has from its beginning had its foundations in the use of cheap, nonunionized labor, white and black, can be characterized, I believe, as a "neocolonial economy." The South has served as a supplier of cheap labor for the production of both raw materials and manufactured goods. Yet, when southern workers buy the finished products, they have to pay the same prices as more highly paid wage earners in other parts of the country. The low wages in Pinetown clearly showed this. The starting wage of the workers ranged from $1.65 to $2.00 per hour with the average wage being $1.80 per hour in 1970. Such low wages are not sufficient, in my opinion, to bring about any major change in the lives of the industrial workers in southern towns.

The average hourly wage of the pulpwood workers was actually higher than that of the manufacturing workers in Pinetown.[25] The pulpwood' workers were paid more than $2.00 per hour. Some of them who worked for efficient producers were paid more than $3.00 per hour. Although the pulpwood workers were paid more than the manufacturing workers on the average per hour, that did not mean that their average yearly income was higher. The higher wages per hour did not help the workers in terms of their long-range plans. They were always worried about the uncertainty of their income. It was difficult for them to calculate their yearly income because of a number of reasons. A good many pulpwood workers were paid by the piece-rate wage system according to their productivity rather than an hourly wage system. Absenteeism occurred frequently. There was a high labor turnover since most of the workers did not stay with the same producer for an entire year. A good many workers were paid in cash, and most of them could not remember how much they were paid. In such cases, the producers did not keep records either. The weather was the most influential factor, however. Workers simply did not know exactly how many days they had actually worked in the previous year and could not know how many days they would be able to work in the coming year.

The poor image of the pulpwood workers held by people in the community, particularly the local merchants, was related to the uncertainty of their incomes. The local merchants rated the pulpwood workers as poor credit risks compared with the manufacturing workers. For instance, when I discussed this with a liquor store owner, he shook his head and told me, "Y' see, I sell lotsa beer to the loggers. My bud'ness depends on doze guys. But I don' like 'em an' I can't believe 'em." The remainder of the merchants in the town similarly indicated the pulpwood workers were irresponsible, and poorer credit risks than the industrial workers.

However, the negative image of the pulpwood workers had begun to change in accordance with changes in the industry. One local forester explained that with today's competitive market the producers invest more capital because they must have sophisticated machines and men who can operate them. Such workers were considered as responsible as manufacturing workers.

In view of changing methods for pulpwood harvesting, small-scale operations could not survive in competition with the larger, better equipped operations. Many producers disbanded their small crews and became workers in the larger crews themselves. One worker and former producer explained the process:

You know, even four or five years ago, if a crew harvested forty or fifty cords of wood per week, it was mighty good. But now, if a producer says his crew could harvest forty cords a week, the damn dealer would laugh at 'im. I couldn' do any better than that 'cause I couldn' put up enough to buy the damn machines. . . . My father was a producer his whole life. I took over the outfit after he died. But hell, the outfit was a couple o' chain-saws an' a truck with a big stick-loader on it. That's what it was all about then. Nowadays, look at them fancy machines.

Indeed, the emphasis on machinery was a consistent topic of conversation among most of the pulpwood workers and producers. I sensed that a "machine-over-man supremacy" attitude pervaded the pulpwood industry. The interest of producers, dealers, and paper company personnel centered on machines rather than the workers. I wondered myself how much the paper companies, including the ones sponsoring our project, would be interested in the nature of human-related studies.

One of the producers who had worked for quite a long time as a producer told me, "[Do] you know why we emphasize machine harvestin' rather than workers? You see, a machine is a dependable laborer, but man is not. A machine performs its job exactly and is never laid off from the job. But we never know when them fellows are goin' to leave us." A producer of a large crew said, "I'm gonna buy a shear [a machine that cut trees at ground level]. Then, I can reduce my men by half. I'll be better off, 'cause I had so many troubles with them guys."

These comments mentally induced me to conduct a comparison of management's views of workers in two quite different cultures, the southern part of Korea and the American South. While conducting a survey of the workers and their attitudes toward trade unions in a Korean cigarette plant in 1963, I found that an unusually high number of manual laborers were employed, although certain machines that were easily obtainable could handle the jobs of many of them. I immediately concluded that the labor must be so cheap as in most developing nations that they could operate more cheaply by hiring the workers than by using expensive machines. However, when I asked the cigarette management head, his response was that, if he could have a choice between ten workers and a machine which has the capacity to take over the ten workers' jobs, he would prefer to choose the workers. He said, "If the machine stopped one day for one reason or another, it would be the same result as if all of the workers had been laid off from their jobs. But it would be very seldom that all of the ten workers stopped from their jobs at once." He also believed that, although one or two workers might be laid off the job, still the rest of the workers could continue to work.

On the surface, the management of the Korean industrial plant appeared to be more trustful of the workers than of the machines. But the reasons for this philosophy extend beyond the economic ramifications of such a policy. Such an attitude made workers feel better and more secure in their jobs. And since management preferred to use machines only when absolutely necessary, workers felt they were needed members of society.

Western journalists observed this philosophy in action during former President Richard Nixon's visit to China. They showed pictures of thousands of Chinese sweeping snow from the streets in Peking without using bulldozers or other snow-sweeping machines. The scene was quite reasonable if one could apply the Oriental way of thinking. Westerners might easily conclude that the government could not afford such equipment, when in reality it was employing its masses of people and helping to maintain their personal dignity.

Considering the different emphasis of management in the pulpwood industry in Pinetown, I decided to put the question to them about whether they would choose the ten workers or a machine which would perform the ten workers' jobs. Most of the producers, except Williams and a few others, whom I met in the Pinetown region opted for the machine. Even those producers who preferred the workers over machines were forced to use more sophisticated machines. In turn, a sizable number of laborers who had maintained their livelihoods by wood-cutting were laid off because a few machine-knowledgeable workers could replace all of them. I could not help but wonder what the pulpwood workers would do as the machines took over their jobs as had only recently happened to farm laborers throughout the South. The more I understood the lives of the pulpwood workers, the more problems I noticed that seemed to envelop their lives. These were unpleasant to contemplate, particularly the knowledge that some men tended to trust more in machines than in their fellow man.

On the morning of October 9, I found a message stuck on my car windshield. I was reminded of the instance of the threat. In fact, the handwriting appeared to be the same as that on the cigarette package. The note was still wet with dewdrops, but I was able to read it. It said, "Come over into the woods near Jim's tree-farm" and was signed "Ed Smith." Swain apparently had persuaded him to cooperate with my study. I will never forget the date. More than six months after I had first contacted him, he was finally convinced of my authenticity and was ready to tell his story. My field note for that day was written thus:

Friday, payday for the pulpwood workers. Blazing sun, hot sands, muggy summer of southern Georgia is almost over, so is the field work. The lone anthropologist finally visits with the lone producer who was never convinced he was an anthropologist. The producer, Ed Smith, grasped a handful of sand and threw it away saying, "Dammit! I shoulda hepcha sooner. I figured what duh white fokes tol' 'bout you wuz right, y' know. I wadn meanin' to be bad or anythin' like that . . . y' know, I jus' can't live like this [pulpwood harvesting as the means of livelihood]. Y' know wha' I mean? It's gettin' worse than the turpentine I used to work at. I can't compete wi' duh udder folkes. I can't buy no machine, y' know. It's jus too 'spensive, y' know. I'm jus' workin' at this and that to keep me up. They say I'm makin' a lotsa money workin' the bank [custodian] and this too. An' they're talkin' about my welfare checks too, y' know. . . ."

He used the colloquial expression of "you know" often in our conversation. However, when he used it, it seemed to me that his "you knows" were not just words thrown away but were meant. I felt as though I did, in fact, understand when he said "you know." I felt quite fortunate indeed to know that I was accepted and trusted by one such as Smith. There was no reason for me to believe in machines rather than men.

My field work with the pulpwood workers in Georgia was significantly more than a simple rite of passage toward becoming a professional anthropologist. It was extremely valuable in two respects.

Personally, I learned much about myself. I was forced to test my personal strengths and weaknesses in order to be able to live alone as an alien in an alien society. Unfortunately, but as is usually the case, I became aware of many of my weaknesses under disturbingly unpropitious conditions. Conversely, I felt I had the right to feel proud of my acceptance by so many, my uncommon-for-me patience, and my successful completion of the project.

Professionally, the field work allowed me the chance to apply the knowledge I had accrued throughout many years of schooling and by living in and learning two cultures. Beyond that, I had to learn to identify for myself the subject matter of the discipline I had chosen for a career. Thus I learned the essence of anthropology, its value, and the vitality of its application.

Having given this intellectual tribute to field work, I must admit I was physically worn out by it and did not feel I should ever desire to employ my time in such a way again. As a matter of fact, during my dissertation defense, one committee member asked me, "What other field work are you planning?" I perceived the question actually to be a not-so-very covert intimation that from now on as an independent anthropologist without faculty supervision I had a professional and personal duty to carry on field work in the areas that I deemed appropriate. I truly felt like saying "no more," because I was tired. I wondered how long other anthropologists needed to recuperate fully between field work experiences.

3

Field Work among
Choctaw Indians

During the summer of 1971, I joined the faculty of the Sociology and Anthropology Department of The University of Tennessee at Martin. Approximately one year later, I was informed by a colleague that a sizable group of American Indians lived within an hour's driving distance of the university. Alluring contemplations of field work came to mind immediately. My enthusiasm for again undertaking such activity surprised me, for it had been less than two years since my previous field work.

Although I have long possessed a genuine curiosity to learn more about American Indians, my knowledge of them was negligible. In fact, I accepted the concept of the "noble savage" (introduced by Rousseau in the 1750s) until I made a trip to the Cherokee reservation in North Carolina in the summer of 1967. At the time, I was a master's level student in sociology and anthropology at Emory University.

At one point, when I asked a motel operator about a good place for trout fishing, he told me I could probably fish in the creek which belonged to the Cherokees because they would think I was Indian. His "common sense" observation startled me, for I had been totally oblivious to our morphological similarities. Belatedly, I realized, the Indians looked like Asians.

The cultural similarities between the Cherokees and rural Korean peasants particularly struck me. Eerie feelings of *déjà vu* crept over me when I spotted a woman carrying a child on her back and a dipper made from a gourd hanging on a wall. For a few moments, I was back in a Korean peasant village, a law school student conducting a survey.

Afterwards, in a North American archaeology class, I was taught for the first time that the American Indians had, in fact, emigrated from Asia—

Siberia.[1] Thereafter, my interest increased as I was exposed throughout my graduate training to the considerable anthropological literature relating to Indians. Even then, I was intrigued with the idea of conducting field work which would allow me to make a comparison of the existing cultural traits of Asians and American Indians.

Since I was familiar with the blacks and whites through my previous field work, I was eager to know something about the reds as well, especially how those remaining in the South fit into the social structure of the South. For some time, I had been irritated by the traditional treatment of the South and southerners by academicians. One source of irritation was the exclusive interest in whites and blacks. There are, in fact, in excess of 75,000 off-reservation, rural Indians in the South. It escapes me how these southern Indians, many of whose ancestors were the original southerners and have lived hundreds and perhaps thousands of years in the South, can be excluded from the category of southerners. Also, the roles of Indians within the general framework of postremoval southern history or in relation to other inhabitants of the southern United States' contemporary scene have attracted little scholarly attention, perhaps being conveniently ignored.[2]

I was anxious to see the responses of the Indians toward an Asian anthropologist. What would be their initial reaction? How would it differ from that of the black and white southerners? Also, since some of the more articulate American Indians have expressed negative attitudes toward white anthropologists,[3] I felt the findings might be an interesting contribution to anthropological field techniques by recording their reaction to a quite different racial identity. As a matter of fact, the candid, unflattering view expressed by Vine Deloria, a Sioux Indian, has substantially tarnished the image of the white anthropologist, whom he described in this way:

Go into any crowd of people. Pick out a tall gaunt white man wearing Bermuda shorts, a World War II Army Air Force flying jacket, an Australian bush hat. . . . He will invariably have a thin sexy wife with stringy hair, an I.Q. of 191, and a vocabulary in which even the prepositions have eleven syllables. . . . This creature is an anthropologist.[4]

I was interested to know whether I would be treated differently in comparison to white anthropologists, since the Indian and I shared morphological similarities. Certainly, I did not fit the stereotype portrayed by Deloria. I am not a tall, gaunt white, but a short, squat yellow.

I was myself as a potential agent for broadening anthropological perspectives by offering a nonwestern view of American Indians. As Roger and Felix Keesing have noted, "anthropology has had to rely far too heavily on stretching the premises, logics, and semantic categories of European experience to fit nonwestern cultures."[5] They suggested that "we urgently need some stretching of the assumptions and categories of other peoples from whose cultures we have sought to learn about human diversity."[6] Those views are definitely applicable in the study of the American Indians.

Along those lines, I have been particularly impressed by the observations of a Chinese anthropologist in 1935, Li An-Che, on Zuni Indians.[7] Although the Zuni were well documented anthropologically, Li was puzzled by several aspects of the almost stereotyped view of Zuni culture held by American anthropologists. He did not share the American understanding of the Zuni religion. Instead of detailing the formal rituals, he attempted to grasp the reverence and depth of feeling beneath the outward formalism. In relation to the Zuni leadership structure, he attempted to correct the misplaced application of American cross-cultural logic which had determined an absence of one. Li explained that "in the competitive Western world . . . where if one does not push ahead, one is surely pushed behind" the absence of ambition implies the absence of leadership, but in another society where mutual give and take is harmoniously assumed among all beings of the world, one might be . . . humble"[8] and still be a leader among men. In this context, leadership is naturally assumed by mutual understanding of all.

Believing that field work with the Indians would be worthwhile, I began to lay the groundwork for its development. By inquiring among students, I was able to find two student informants from the county seat, Toptown. My department arranged my schedule with class meetings only three days per week so that I could devote the other days to field work. Also, I was joined during this early stage by a history faculty member, who was interested in the histories of ethnic groups.

From one student, I learned that the Indians were Choctaws. They lived and worked as farm laborers in the lowlands along the Mississippi River. Whether or not the group was affiliated directly with the Choctaws in Mississippi or Oklahoma was not known.

As I have pointed out already, I possessed only a meager knowledge of American Indians in general, but of the Choctaws I had a little better notion. Bailey, my major professor at Georgia, had done his field work among the Choctaw Indians in 1962. Also, several of my former colleagues in graduate school wrote theses and dissertations under his supervision relating to the Choctaws.[9] One of them, John H. Peterson, Jr., was then serving as the chief planner for the tribal government of the Mississippi Band of Choctaw Indians. I was very pleased to know that I could get information and assistance from them.

The first student with whom I talked did not have a very positive attitude toward the Choctaws. He thought they looked weird—which, incidentally, made me wonder what he thought of me. He had once gotten lost in the lowlands and was scared when he came upon the Choctaws. Apparently, he had the notion that if people look different, they may be dangerous. The notion is what is dangerous. My curiosity was greatly aroused when he mentioned "white owners" of the Choctaw. He said I should contact the Choctaws through them. He promised to give me additional information later but never returned to my office.

The second student, Ken Johnson, a part-time reporter for the county newspaper, seemed more knowledgeable and observant. However, he would not impart his knowledge to me directly. He considered himself a local historian. In fact, he was preparing a manuscript of the history of Toptown for publication. When asked, he hinted that the story of the Choctaw was not worth including. He seemed to identify with my historian friend and wanted to demonstrate his knowledge to me. With the historian, he would talk freely even in my presence. Thus only by working with the historian was I able to obtain the information. The reason for this peculiar discrimination was not immediately discernible, but none of the reasons I could think of were positive.

Johnson told us the Choctaws had emigrated from Mississippi and recollected that the size of the Choctaw population had reached three hundred or more in the early 1960s. He estimated that one hundred Choctaws remained. He understood that the Choctaw Indians were known to be a very peaceful group of people who seldom bothered the other inhabitants, which included blacks and whites. In the past, they had worn their native costumes and displayed their culture each year at the county fair. They still would come to Toptown almost every weekend to purchase goods. Several families would make the trip together in one car. Although each Choctaw individual might have different business in town, everyone would wait until the others finished their affairs. The ones who finished before the others would gather and wait at a certain corner of the county courthouse square to see and to be seen. We were told that if anyone went to that corner of the courthouse square around 2:00 P.M. on any Saturday, he would see Choctaws standing there. Seemingly, in order to enhance his reputation with us and his journalistic peers, Johnson suggested that we come to Toptown sometime in January as his guests. He promised to give us a grand tour of Toptown via the newspaper office and to take us to Riverville as well.

While still preparing for the field work, I found myself facing a practical problem. Since the proposed field work would require a great deal of information about the reservation as well as Riverville, I would need to drive over 300 miles to reach the reservation in east central Mississippi. I could not make the round trip daily and collect much data. So, I began to wonder how I might cover the minimum expenses.

Ironically, on several occasions while in southern Georgia, I had thought about conducting field work by paying my own expenses. This I felt would be possible when I got a job and would provide me freedom from the usual guidelines of funding agents. In my experience, such guidelines had led to frustrations and seriously limited the field work, particularly through timetables. I now know it is highly unlikely that any faculty member could ever support his own field expenses.

After several unsuccessful attempts to obtain funds from the funding agencies, I was supported from the departmental operating budget. The chairman of my department was very enthusiastic about the proposed field work, and his encouragement greatly facilitated the preliminary stage of the field work.

My patience could not wait until January to go with Johnson to Riverville. So, one Saturday morning in early November 1972, my family and I took off for a pioneering trip to Riverville via Toptown. I wanted a general sense of the village and its vicinity, such as spatial distances, road conditions, and the time consumed by driving back and forth from the university to Riverville. Most of all, I wanted to confirm the reliability of Johnson's information. My wife and two sons willingly joined me for the trip. Thus our entourage was intended to appear as a family outing to curious onlookers.

The road time to Toptown was no more than an hour and a half, which meant I could conveniently make the trip daily. Toptown was almost the stereotype of a southern county seat in the old tradition, with the county courthouse in the center of the town and the business district arranged around the courthouse square.[10] As we circled the square, my boys shouted, "There's one." Indeed, three Indians stood on a corner.

Other than the Indians there was nothing out of the ordinary about Toptown, except its large population of blacks and its hilliness.[11] I had thought that since it was so close to the Mississippi River that it would be located on flat or lower-lying land. But it is located in hills ranging from 300 to 350 feet in elevation.

As we drove toward the Mississippi River and Riverville, the elevation suddenly dropped about halfway from Toptown and leveled off to almost the level of the river. The paved road got narrower. The brick and well-painted wooden houses along the route were outnumbered by dilapidated, worn-out shacks in critical need of repair. But regardless of their shapes, sizes or building materials, all houses were on stilts. That was a quaint custom to us tourists. I could imagine the hardships endured, however, when water reached those houses.

Soon the paved road ended and a dirt road began. I sensed I was near the village where the Indians resided. At the entrance of Riverville, I saw a well-kept Baptist Church, which I later learned had been built by student volunteers from The University of Tennessee at Martin in the early 1960s. There was little semblance to a town with only a handful of houses and a grocery. The blacks appeared to outnumber the Choctaws and whites combined. Within the apparent boundaries of Riverville, I saw only one Choctaw family. I had thought of Riverville as a small village in which the Choctaw Indians resided side by side, isolated from the blacks and whites. Instead, the Choctaw house that I saw was located next to a white residence. On the other side of the road were a number of shacks in which blacks lived. There appeared to be no real residential segregation by the three racial groups. Their relationship appeared to be a symbiotic one.

As we continued along the dirt road, I realized we were actually driving alongside the Mississippi River. One could easily see the water from the road because there was no levee. Having only its natural bank, the river could flood the flatland without resistance whenever it rose.

At this point, I should redefine Riverville. In the minds of the natives, it was not just the small settlement around the grocery but began there and included a four-square-mile area beyond that stretched along the Mississippi River. Thus Riverville was not a village but what natives preferred to call a community.[12] Ecologically, this is correct.

I gained more information than I had anticipated on that brief tour. The dangers described by my first student informant were a figment of his imagination. No one paid particular attention to us as we toured the community. The trip gave me a grasp of the general way of life and presented some possibilities for study. I wanted to learn more about the life patterns of the Choctaws, their relations as an ethnic group in a tri-ethnic setting dominated by blacks and whites, their relations to the Choctaws on the reservation in Mississippi, and the extent of their participation in the social institutions of the county as a whole. In addition, I was curious about the leading factors influencing their emigration to Riverville because it contrasted with the urbanization trends in American society. Why did these Choctaws adopt a rural life pattern while many other reservation Indians went to the cities?

Although a good many writers, predominantly anthropologists, have written about the off-reservation Indians, they have failed to offer appropriate information dealing with the Indians in rural communities. Most of the available information is related to urban life.[13] In a report prepared in 1969 for the Joint Economic Committee of the U. S. Congress, Helen Johnson described the very limited ethnographic information on off-reservation rural Indians:

No person or agency at the present time has the requisite knowledge to report on their current social-economic situation with precision. It is believed that many groups are in poverty, in poor health, in poor housing . . . . Detailed local knowledge about them is absolutely required in order to ensure that such assistance is given intelligently and with understanding.[14]

On Saturday morning, January 20, 1973, my historian colleague and I were scheduled to meet Johnson, the part-time reporter of the county newspaper, at his office in Toptown. This was the appointed date for his promised tour. We were led into the office where Johnson introduced his senior reporter to us. Then he introduced my colleague as "Dr. So-and-so," explaining who he was. The senior reporter shook hands with him. However, I was not given an introduction. My colleague realized this and quickly responded explaining about me. The man made no move to shake hands. In order to see his reaction, I offered my hand. But he avoided it awkwardly by turning his head away. The historian was greatly disturbed by the scene. Since he was a historian, he had no experience in field work. He had not considered the possibility that the native lay-intellectual might reject a researcher of a different ethnicity.

The senior reporter's long association with the local newspaper meant he would be a key informant if he would be cooperative. But his attitude indicated that as far as I was involved in the project, he would not reveal any information. As we toured the facilities of the office, the historian asked me how I could stand such treatment. I explained that this was common in the field. Further, we would not get assistance from such local intellectuals, because they usually do not like anyone from university circles.

The cold treatment which I received from the senior reporter of the Toptown newspaper made me aware that my occupation could be a disadvantage in the field. Since my colleague had introduced me as a university faculty member, the senior reporter had thought that I was an American instead of a foreigner. I have observed among southerners the necessity for determining the difference between a member of a minority group and a foreigner. As long as a foreigner is obviously a foreigner, they see him as a foreigner. But if a foreigner has succeeded in America and appears to be American, then they treat him as a member of a minority group. If I had been introduced as a foreign student helping with the project, then the senior reporter might have been friendly or at least tolerant.

I sensed that the historian and I would have problems working together. The historian expected to locate a great deal of information in the library, whereas I wanted to get into the field. That was natural because his training as a historian had made him more interested in the library than in the field. However, the real problem for me was not in our different training, but rather in the attention of the townspeople. Whenever we did talk with the natives, they preferred to talk to him. I remained in his shadow. I seldom had a chance to ask questions. I realized his presence was disadvantageous for my field work.

Before we left the town for Riverville, we were able to obtain copies of two fairly recent feature articles of a newspaper about the Choctaws. One reported the death of a seventy-four-year-old Choctaw woman. The whites in Toptown had considered her the chief of Riverville Choctaws. She appeared to be well respected, as evidenced by a huge color portrait of her hanging on the wall of a local photo shop. The librarian said she had been the best known of the Choctaw Indians. Johnson added that she was known so well because she never spoke English, never talked to whites, and never visited Toptown. The other article which had been written earlier was a feature story about the Riverville Choctaw. It contained a description of the "female chief":

Her face is brown and creased from the sun that waits at the end of thousands of cotton rows. Her hands have worn out many hoes, woven countless baskets and worked a myriad of colored beads into splashes of decoration. English does not pass her lips . . . uses only Choctaw, the language of her ancestors; spoken with hard emphasis on the vowels, like a harsh wind beating through a cane-grown river bottom.[15]

As we traveled to Riverville, Johnson gave us a general background of the Choctaw Indians in Riverville. According to him, it would be very difficult to determine the size of the Choctaw population in Riverville, because they were seasonal migrants. Many Choctaw Indians would stay in Riverville during the farming season and return to the reservation for the off-season. Also, a good many were temporary migrants who lived in Riverville for irregular periods of time before returning to the reservation or going elsewhere. There had been a drastic reduction in the Choctaw population during the off-farming season, usually the months of November, December, January, and February. He assured us that we would see more Choctaws if we returned in March.

If that was true, an unfortunate irony existed. The very time of the Choctaws' return coincided with the seasonal floods. After the ice belt of the upper tributaries of the Mississippi River in the northern states had melted, the increased water level often caused spring floods, especially in low-lying areas with no levee such as Riverville. Yet, many of the Choctaws were gone during the periods of safety from the flood. Indeed, in the latter part of March 1973, I was able to observe the worst flood they had ever recorded. At that time, all of Riverville and its vicinity was covered by the Mississippi River. Several Choctaw Indians who were on the scene told me they were used to the flooding. They commented that although the entire county has been known as a "cotton county," cotton could not be planted in the lowlands. After the flood water resided, not enough time would remain in

the growing season for the soil to dry out and the cotton to mature. Thus
soybeans are usually planted on most of that land. The seasonal floods did
bring natural fertilizer to the land. This greater fertility at one time had
promised the Choctaw Indians higher incomes. But it was a miserable scene
for me to watch the entire community under flood water.

Johnson's logical, detailed outline of seasonal migration proved later to
be inaccurate. As a result, in my field work, I de-emphasized the lay
opinions of whites and sought information from Choctaws. I was determined to contact the Choctaw Indians directly. If I went through white
channels, unnecessary publicity might result and divert the field work.
Furthermore, I did not want to develop assumptions about the Choctaws
through familiarization with any stereotyped images of the Indians, such as
those the one student informant had advocated. Having studied whites and
blacks previously, I wished to emphasize the Indians only. Despite the
potential for studying the tri-ethnic relations of the Indians, whites, and
blacks, I wanted to understand those relationships through the eyes of the
Indians. I resolved to maintain courteous relationships with whites such as
Johnson but to avoid them when possible. Since I did not plan to get much
information on the whites in Toptown and the county, their welcome was
not a serious matter, but I felt their understanding of my occupation was
essential. I wanted clear identification that I came as a researcher from a
university rather than as an employee of the federal government, a civil
rights worker, or an activist. Thus upon my request, an official of The
University of Tennessee at Martin wrote a letter of introduction to some
leading citizens of the county.

In order to find out how many Choctaws remained in Riverville during
the off-farming season, I wanted to count them before March. My colleague
and I contacted a female teacher, who was introduced by Johnson, of
Toptown High School. Choctaw students attended there because it was the
only high school in the county, although it was more than 15 miles away
from their homes. The teacher was cooperative and set a date for us to meet
the Choctaw students in her office.

In late February when we were scheduled to meet the Choctaw students
in their high school, we arrived earlier than we had anticipated. So, we
visited a local librarian for a casual conversation. She was as kind and cordial
as she had been previously, but did not want to talk about the Choctaws.
She answered a couple of questions, then became noncommittal. Her

taciturnity bothered me and awakened me to the likelihood that the intention of the official's letters had misfired. The letters may have served to call attention to me rather than to obtain cooperation, with the net result of the addressees choosing to shield their community from the prying of an outsider. I believed I had made a mistake. I can never ascertain the proper methods for conducting field work. The field is a natural laboratory in which one has little control of variables other than one's own involvement. With each circumstance so varied, there can be no uniform rules. Yet, one's choice of field methods dictates the success or failure of one's field work. I would say that wise choice can only come by experience.

I feared the teacher's attitude might have changed, also. However, two Choctaw students, Linda and Mary, were waiting for us in her office. The teacher explained to her Choctaw pupils that we were interested in the history and culture of the Choctaw Indians in Riverville. They seemed to understand our purpose clearly. As we talked, they showed interest in my appearance. They seemed to prefer talking to me rather than to my colleague. About that time, my colleague jokingly told the Choctaw students, "He's a Navajo Indian, you know." I agreed that I was. They accepted that unquestioningly. But when the teacher expressed her amazement, I quickly retracted and told them that I was an Oriental, a Korean. Everybody laughed together. We all agreed that the Indians and Orientals were quite similar in physical appearance. The mood in the office had become very relaxed.

I told them I was interested in knowing about the culture of the Choctaws and the culture of the American Indians as a whole. I asked about the possibility of arranging a meeting with their parents. Both assured me their parents would willingly meet me. In fact, they seemed anxious for such a meeting. I got the impression I would be a topic of conversation with parents and neighbors.

During the course of our conversation, I was struck by some remarkable cultural similarities between the Choctaws and Koreans, perhaps the Orientals as a whole. For instance, when I inquired about the number of Choctaws in the area, Linda answered that there were "about ten of 'em." This estimate surprised her teacher who immediately pointed out that the numbers of Mary's and Linda's families exceeded ten. However, the estimate had seemed quite reasonable to me because I automatically think in terms of the numbers of extended families. It turned out that the Choctaws do as well, for Linda continued by reciting the different family names. It seemed ironic to me that although neither of us was speaking in our native tongue, we were actually relating to and understanding each other through some cultural similarities. Since I was raised in a similar cultural niche with a strong sense of extended family, I had little difficulty in understanding what Linda had meant.

Afterwards, the counselor identified Linda as the granddaughter of the so-called female chief. According to her, Linda's father had taken over the leadership of the Choctaws in Riverville after his mother's death. The teacher had intentionally selected Linda for us. She had felt this would make contacting the rest of the Choctaws easy. I just hoped Linda's father would go along with the proposed meeting. The teacher gave me a brief background of him. He was working as a tenant farmer for a white, who owned a sizable farm in the Riverville vicinity. He had been working for Harding for more than ten years.

This was the first time I realized that the local school teachers could serve as good informants for field work in a small community. Having a college education, they understand what research is all about, and that it is not likely to be harmful to the community. Although seldom outspoken or visible, they are often the true intellectuals in their community. They usually differ greatly from the lay-intellectuals, are quite tolerant, and want to be helpful.

The appointment with Linda's father was for March 3. He would expect to meet me around two o'clock at the Riverville grocery store. The historian accompanied me. Frankly, had I been going to meet a white, I would probably have chosen to leave without him. But since I was going to meet Indians, I felt very positive about his coming along.

When we arrived at the store, I saw an old model pickup truck parked in front of the store. A middle-aged man stood outside. He was dressed fully in a native Choctaw costume with a bright-red top, plain black trousers, and a beaded necklace. It was the first time I had seen a Choctaw Indian's costume.

I introduced myself to Linda's father, John Thompson. Then, before I could introduce my colleague, Thompson asked me to ride in his pickup truck and let my colleague drive my car. I hopped into his truck without any hesitation, because I thought he had something to say privately. Indeed, he did. He asked, "Who's that white man?" I told him he was a good friend of mine and not to worry about him. I began to explain about my interest and occupation. But he quickly hinted that there was no need for such explanations. He trusted me completely. That certainly made me feel good.

Thompson's English was guttural and abrupt, yet to me it was clear and understandable. Some of his explanations were only partial and incomplete. But I did not feel any barriers between us. I asked him to provide a general knowledge about the Choctaw people in Riverville for me, including the history of their migration. However, he was more interested in learning about me than in talking to me about Choctaws.

He suggested that we drive around the community in order to get a general idea of Riverville spatially. The road circling the locality is called Four Miles, because it is a square consisting of four one-mile segments. He stopped in front of a worn-out shack and told me that it was where he had lived when he had first moved to Riverville with his mother. She had finished her life there. He was sentimental about the house and wished he could afford to preserve it. If one more flood came, he said, it would be washed away by the river. The shack was probably the worst one I had ever seen throughout my entire field work in the American South.

Thompson paid little attention to my colleague and seldom talked to him. I noticed he had the same feeling which I had experienced while he was talking to Toptown whites. I really felt that I should probably contact the Indians without him or any other white friend so that the Choctaws would feel more comfortable. I was very encouraged by Thompson's warm reception and friendly treatment. I became confident that I as an Oriental who looked like the Indians would indeed have some advantages over a white anthropologist.

Our most notable discussion took place in the home of Thompson's cousin. As we pulled off the road in front of the house, I asked him about the row of shacks along the other side of the road. He answered, "Those's coloreds." Parenthetically, in Riverville there was a racial hierachy in accordance with the darkness of skin color. My colleague and I were led inside through the back door and passed through a bedroom in which I noticed a twenty-three-inch color television set. As I came into the living room, I was surprised to see another color television set, a rather expensive-looking stereo system, and a bed. The room served the dual purposes of living room and bedroom. Oddly enough, in contrast to the color television and the stereo, the room was heated by an old, woodburning, potbellied stove.

The family members joined the conversation. I asked about and was told their backgrounds and the stories of their migrations. As our conversation progressed, the Choctaws became the anthropologists and I the respondent. They kept asking questions about Orientals and their cultures. A young man, Dezmon Thompson, who was on leave from military duty, was the most active questioner. It seemed to me that they had been preparing questions for me ever since Linda had told them I was coming. When Dezmon tired, others would ask questions. Occasionally, they would discuss a question among themselves in Choctaw before they would ask it of me.

Since I looked similar to them, they became curious to find out any cultural similarities. They began to compare our languages. They asked me how I addressed my parents, siblings, and other close relatives. They explained their kinship terms and spelled them. Of course, we were unable to find any term which was common for both Choctaw and Korean. Dezmon's mother wanted to check for any similarities between Choctaw and Korean music. At his mother's prompting, Dezmon asked me to sing a Korean song. I told them that I was not prepared to do that. I asked them to sing. We all laughed. Finally, they turned on the stereo and played a song, entitled "Choctaw Saturday Night." It sounded like American popular music. I later learned that the text of the song was written by my friend who used to work on the Choctaw reservation in Mississippi. I told them that I would bring an album of Korean music on my next trip to Riverville.

Lady Thompson, who did not speak to me in English, brought her collection of Choctaw artifacts, mostly beadwork. She showed me a stick to be used in their traditional stickball game and said in Choctaw, "ishtabolli," which was the name of the stick. Later, she brought several letters with U.S. military stamps. Thompson quickly joined in the conversation and wanted to explain the letters. The older brother of Dezmon, Harry, had joined the military and was stationed in Korea.

I read several of Harry's letters from Korea in which he described how the Korean peasants were similar to the Choctaw farm laborers. He indicated that he was impressed by the Korean people and especially by the similarities. He had learned a few Korean words and had written them in his letter. His family asked me to write to him, explain who I was, and to introduce my relatives in Korea to him. I did this but we never established an ongoing exchange. Two years later, while I was directing the manpower survey, my research assistant who surveyed the Choctaws in West Tennessee told me that Harry was scheduled to be honorably discharged from military service. He did not return to the home I visited, however. It had been washed away by the floods. The family had relocated in the hills near Toptown.

Thompson later took us to meet his family. His wife and two daughters were working on Choctaw crafts, mostly beadwork. As early migrants, they knew most of the events in the history of the Choctaws of Riverville. Although they had been there for twenty years, they still maintained close ties with the Choctaws on the reservation in Mississippi.

As my colleague and I headed home, foremost in my mind was the knowledge of receptiveness of the Choctaws to an Asian. I could not have hoped for a better response. This encouraged me to pursue the idea of contacting the Choctaws on the reservation in Mississippi.

Discussing the day's events, I jokingly commented to my colleague, "I think I can take care of the Indians and you can take care of the whites. But, what about the blacks?" Yet, it was not altogether a joke. I was actually handicapped by his presence when Thompson was telling that he was still a sharecropper for a white landowner but refused to comment further. I decided then that in the future I should contact the Choctaws alone.

I continued my participant-observation of the Choctaws in Riverville on most Tuesdays, Thursdays, and weekends until I had gained an understanding of their life patterns. Most of my effort had been spent in determining the type of the community in relation to the reservation as well as the community's relationship to the white-dominated Toptown.

Meanwhile, I contacted my friend, John H. Peterson, Jr., who was the chief planner at the tribal office on the reservation in Mississippi, in order to initiate research there with former residents of West Tennessee. He told me he would like to discuss the matter with me at the joint meeting of the Southern Anthropological Society and the American Ethnological Society in Wrightsville Beach, North Carolina. In that meeting, he was scheduled to present a paper jointly with a Choctaw Indian, the vice-chairman of the tribal council of the Mississippi Band of Choctaw Indians, who had lived in Riverville during his boyhood. We both felt he would be the most valuable informant I could contact among reservation Choctaws who had once lived in Riverville.

The meeting was held in early March and endured the lingering winds and chills of winter. My purpose in attending was primarily to meet the vice-chairman of the tribal council and to ask for his assistance. I was unable to meet him prior to the presentation of his paper. The room of the session in which his paper was scheduled to be delivered was packed. Since an American Indian was scheduled to present a paper, a good many anthropologists were interested in what he would present. His presentation was remarkably good and well received. After the session, many anthropologists lined up to meet him. I left the line without meeting him when one anthropologist asked me, "Are you a Choctaw Indian, too?"

That evening I was able to set up a private talk with him. He seemed very surprised to meet an Asian anthropologist among the many American anthropologists. He admitted that he was not quite comfortable around the American anthropologists. Nevertheless, as the Choctaws in Riverville had been, he was at ease with me. He manifested his interest in meeting an anthropologist who physically resembled him. After a few beers and more talk, we were addressing each other by our first names.

I asked him about his motivation for becoming involved in the politics of the reservation. He answered that it had been an outgrowth of his years in Riverville. He said, "Believe it or not, I flunked out of the eighth grade when I entered Toptown Junior High. It was because I could not understand English very well. Well, I dropped out of school and picked cotton in the fields near Riverville. While I was picking the cotton, I thought about me and my people a lot. I thought a lot about what I could do for myself and could do for my people." He came to a conclusion that he should have a proper education. He said he knew he could not get an adequate education if he stayed in Riverville. So, he ran away from home and returned to the reservation. He was fourteen years old at the time. He stayed for a while with his grandparents and entered the Choctaw Central School. Eventually, his strong desire for education led him all the way through four years of college. He confessed that if he had stayed in Riverville he would have turned out to be a sharecropper for the whites.

Although he was a young, educated Indian, he was not particularly rebellious toward the white-dominated mainstream of American culture.

Rather, he was a realistic, pragmatic, Indian politician. He admitted the problems facing the Indians and believed the only way truly to improve the lives of the Indians was through education. As a matter of fact, when I later conducted the social, economic, and demographic study of the entire Choctaw population, he was no longer the vice-chairman of the tribal council because he had resigned and enrolled in graduate school at a university to work on a master's degree in education.

When I asked his assistance in extending field work to the reservation, he assured me of his maximum cooperation. He added that basically he did not like to see too many anthropologists around the reservation plaguing the Choctaws. However, he would be available to assist any study that was advantageous for his people. Fortunately for me, he felt my proposed study would be useful.

When I asked him about a proper time for visiting the reservation, he suggested that I come during the annual Choctaw fair for several reasons. He said that during the fair virtually all tribal government operations would be in recess, so he could spend most of his time helping me. He mentioned that many off-reservation Choctaws, particularly those from Riverville, would attend. Also, during the fair, he thought I would not arouse the suspicion of local whites because they would naturally assume that I was a tourist. He warned me that if I were thought to be a civil rights worker or an activist of some kind, I would be in danger.

I was pleased to know that my association with him was not formal or superficial but a genuine one. He even worried about my safety. My trip to the meeting had truly been successful if only in making his acquaintance.

Eventually, in order to assess the relationship between the Choctaws on the reservation and the Choctaws in Riverville, I made several trips to the reservation located in east central Mississippi. As a result, I became acquainted with the officials of the tribal government. Their general attitude toward me was warm and friendly. As at Riverville, they expressed interest in my resemblance to themselves. There was a general lack of resentment to my being an anthropologist.

Apparently, they did not think of me as the kind of anthropologist portrayed by Eileen Maynard when she said, "They are prone to consider the anthropologists as a predator who is using the Indian to further his career, i.e., as a stepping stone to an academic degree or as a way of proving material so he can add another publication feather to his professional bonnet."[16] Although often curious about me, they did not display suspicion and seemed to accept me as one interested in American Indians because of our similar backgrounds.

The Choctaws living in Riverville and its vicinity began migrating there in 1952. During the course of labor recruitment, white landowners in the Riverville area brought a number of Choctaws from the Neshoba County area in Mississippi, which is heavily populated by the Mississippi Band of Choctaw Indians.[17] The movement of the Choctaws from Mississippi to West Tennessee was primarily based on their search for better economic opportunities. The lower-lying area around Riverville was introduced to the Choctaws in Mississippi as a "land of opportunity."

In the 1950s, the economic outlook in Mississippi, particularly near the Choctaw Indian reservation, steadily worsened.[18] The decline of small farming operations owing to changes in farming methods and the decline of sharecropping became major "push" factors for the Choctaws to move away from the reservation.[19] At the same time, the labor recruitment made by Riverville landowners because of a labor shortage became an attractive "pull" factor for many Choctaws who intended to move away from the reservation to seek jobs elsewhere.[20] As a result, the Choctaw migration to Riverville took place by the interaction of these "push" and "pull" factors.[21] Thus they formed a semi-reservation rural community in Riverville, which was known then as a Choctaw community being established by the Mississippi Band of the Choctaw Indians.

The migration of the Mississippi Band of Choctaw Indians to Riverville had a special meaning for the Choctaws living on the reservation. It provided them with an alternative to the dire economic conditions on the reservation. Also, for the first time, they knew their sharecropping way of life was in demand outside the reservation area. They took the job offer made by the landowners in Riverville without any hesitation because the job required no specific skill. Their destination was another rural setting which would not require nearly so much adjustment as a city would. Soon after the migration of the first group, other families heard positive news through the kinship network of relatives in Riverville.

At one time there were more than 300 Choctaws in Riverville and its immediate vicinity. Available records estimated the population of the Choctaws in Riverville at 200 in 1960. But by 1967, the Choctaw population had decreased significantly.[22] A good many of the Choctaws returned to the reservation. In recent years, the population has remained stable.[23]

The transplanted Choctaws in Riverville regarded themselves as a single people defined by common language, customs, origin, and appearance, as distinct from the rest of the people in Riverville and its vicinity. Because they migrated along the line of their kinship network, most are closely related. One young Choctaw male confided that he would have a difficult time acquiring a spouse because most available Choctaw girls were his cousins. Of course, this was true for his female counterparts as well. Besides going to Toptown as customers, the Choctaws' interaction with the rest of society was limited. Their contacts with whites usually related to shopping or to their jobs.

A major event each year was the annual sharecropping agreement. Usually, they would reach an agreement whereby the sharecroppers would be furnished with seed and equipment to raise certain crops. Half of the income from the sale of the crops minus the cost of insecticides would go to the sharecroppers. In addition to this, while the landowners were assured of reliable labor, loyalty, and some other personal favors, the sharecroppers would receive credit and protection.[24]

The associations of Choctaws with blacks were few, if not exceptional. They tended to look down on blacks, calling them "colored people." This social distance is reflected in their pattern of interracial marriages. While there had been several marriages between Choctaws and whites, no marriages between Choctaws and blacks had ever occurred in Riverville and its vicinity. Monte Kenaston has also observed the behavior of Choctaws toward blacks and found "no one who would admit to having any kind of more than temporary relationship to a Negro, male or female, as a friend or as sexual object. It is not that one should not marry a Negro; rather, the attitude is that no one could possibly want to do so."[25]

Although Kenaston maintains that the migration of the Choctaws to Riverville had improved their financial position, I found this difficult to judge. I also found difficulty in determining the economic status of families because one set of material cultural items could not serve as criteria for making such a judgment. Some families had potbellied stoves and outdoor toilets, but also had large color television sets and expensive stereos. In some cases, a family would not have decent housing, yet maintained a luxurious automobile. Their personal assets often included refrigerators, sewing machines, television sets, and automobiles. Yet most of these material items were also common to the Choctaws on the reservation.[26] It was apparent, however, that the income of the sharecroppers in Riverville was so low that the bulk of the household budget went for food. Whatever was left after buying food and paying bills usually went for beer, clothing, and gas. They were total consumers who left no room for saving to invest in the improvement of their future.

The Choctaw community was controlled by the white establishment, particularly the white landowners. At the same time, they were virtually independent of the tribal government on the reservation in Mississippi. They did not really expect much support from it. Nor did they feel the necessity for developing their own leadership. Thompson was well respected and often called "chief" by local whites. But he flatly denied chieftain status when I inquired about it.

When I was in the final stage of my field work, the tribal government of the Mississippi Band of Choctaw Indians appointed a health representative for West Tennessee Choctaws. His primary job was as liaison between the tribal government community-health service and the Choctaws in the Riverville area. Incidentally, the post was created after I had repeatedly called the attention of tribal government officials to the problems of Choctaws in West Tennessee.[27]

Of course, Riverville Choctaws were bound together by their common cultural heritage. The female Choctaws continued to make native costumes without any commercial purpose in mind. The Choctaw identity was further secured by their marriage pattern. Although interracial marriage was not desirable, they were more tolerant of marriage between Choctaw females and white males than of reverse cases.[28] At Riverville, there had been two cases of interracial marriage between Choctaw females and white males. It is my personal speculation that they believed the offspring born to Choctaw females and white males would maintain a Choctaw cultural heritage, because the children would be enculturated mainly by the mother. In addition to this, Choctaws maintain a matrilineal and matriarchal society.[29]

Despite affection for their native culture, the Choctaws in Riverville were in the process of adapting to the white culture (the "high culture" from their frame of reference). They spoke the Choctaw language among themselves, but English was not ignored.[30] They no longer wore native costumes, except on special occasions, such as at county fairs. They attended Christian churches and sent their children to white schools. Their acculturation was more visible than that of Choctaws on the reservation in Mississippi.

Most Riverville Choctaws were in the process of losing their original kinship terms. Hence as far as terminology was concerned, their kinship system was changing.[31] Many traditional kinship terms had been replaced by personal names. Due to acculturation, the dominant form of family type had become the nuclear family common to white Americans. Acculturation has been described by two researchers, one a Choctaw himself, in this way:

. . . as a result of living in the rural South, the Southern Indians have adopted many cultural traits which are often attributed to rural southerners, both White and Black. . . . The Southern Baptist Church is the largest and most active religious denomination among the Choctaws. Corn bread and pork form important parts of the Choctaw diet. Choctaw women make quilts and until recently most Choctaw men wore bib overalls. Even the spoken English of most Choctaws bears a heavy Southern accent. A few years ago, a western Indian visitor to Mississippi asked jokingly, "Are you sure you guys aren't rednecks instead of redskins?"[32]

The more I got to know about the Choctaw community in Riverville, the more interested I became in the structure of Riverville. It seemed to be a partial society, structurally and culturally. However, in order to understand further about its structural and cultural semiautonomy, I checked their relations to the reservation. There was some indication that the Choctaw cultural heritage had been reinforced by their contacts with the reservation.

The result of contact with the reservation indicated that the officials of the Choctaw tribal government were fully aware of the existence of the Choctaws in Riverville, but no formal relationship between them existed. According to the Social Service Branch of the Choctaw Agency, Bureau of Indian Affairs, they did not provide any social services for the Choctaws in Riverville, except medical service during their visits to the reservation. An official of the medical records section in the Choctaw service unit of the U.S. Public Health Service gave this reply to my question about the medical service for the Riverville Choctaws:

Most of 'em were 'riginally from Bogue Chitto, and so unless they say so, we don't know if they're from Tennessee or permanent residents here. If they mention they're from Tennessee, I mark their medical records, but since we don't make a special effort to fin' out where they're currently livin', it'd be difficult to tell. . . . They move 'round a lot, you know. I think some of 'em come by when they're visitin' relatives here. And, there're some who catch a bus to come down for treatment. John Robinson, for example, is a diabetic and needs regular care, so we see 'im regularly. And, there're one or two who come down to have their babies delivered.

The official quoted above indicated that when the Choctaws returned to the reservation, they received full benefits as Choctaw Indians. Their membership within the tribe had nothing to do with current residence but was determined simply by consanguineal relationships. As a hypothetical assumption, there would likely be an increasing rate of interracial marriages between the Choctaws and the non-Choctaws in the future, particularly in off-reservation settings. The lack of explicit regulations for membership in the tribe will likely bring about complicated cases in the future. Eventually, if one claims to be a Choctaw, there will be no clear criteria to verify or deny the claim, since the tribe does not possess a written genealogy containing all identifiable Choctaws. Compiling a genealogy will become more difficult as each member of the older generation of Choctaws passes away. .

Later, I learned that the major contact between the reservation and off-reservation Choctaws had been made through their kinship network. Despite changes in the kinship system, including the terminology, Choctaws were still strongly tied to their relatives. Their duties, obligations, and other social relationships centered around their kinship system. They were noticeably closer to their kin than the average white Americans. As a matter of fact, the older Choctaws retained the original kinship terms, whereas the younger ones did not use them often or at all.

Indeed, the classification of the Choctaw kinship system would be dependent upon whom an anthropologist asked to define the terms. Different informants given their background would indicate a different kinship typology. The original Choctaw kinship system was unilineal with the matrilineal system having moieties, but now a bilateral system is developing.[33]

The Choctaws in Riverville attend the funerals of their kin on the reservation. Since almost all of the Riverville Choctaws are related to each other bilaterally, a large portion of the Riverville Choctaws go to the reservation to attend the same funeral. Also, according to Kenaston, if a non-infant Choctaw in Riverville died, the dead body would be sent to the reservation for burial.[34] It is doubtful that anyone among Riverville Choctaws would admit that their traveling to a funeral on the reservation was for the purpose of renewing their kinship ties and fostering their traditional kinship system. However, the consequences were just that. Indeed, the Choctaw out-migration had been arranged through this kinship channel. And this is still the case. A good many Choctaws believed the kinship channel was more efficient and reputable for finding jobs than the various employment agencies.

Upon considering the information given above, I concluded that the Choctaw village in Riverville was a peasant village structurally. The community was structurally located between the tribal Choctaws on the reservation and urban whites in Toptown. This type of semiautonomous village has been identified as peasant—part-society by Lloyd Fallers.[35] Besides the structural ties, as George Foster has suggested, other characteristics are essential for determining the peasant status, such as social, economic, religious, and cultural aspects of a community.[36]

As described already, since the income of the Choctaw sharecroppers was so low, no investment could be made to improve their future lives. Such an economy is also considered to be semiautonomous.[37] The Choctaws in Riverville had never developed a leadership structure. They were controlled by the whites. The culture of the Choctaws in Riverville was exactly the same as that which Fallers noted[38] when he said:

The peasant, accepting the standards of the high culture to some degree, to that degree also accepts its judgment of him as ignorant and uncouth. At the same time, he possesses his own folk culture, containing high culture elements, and this provides him with an independent basis for a sense of self-esteem, together with an ideology within which he may express his partial hostility toward the elite and its version of the common culture.[39]

The Choctaws in Riverville shared the native Choctaw culture, yet they had begun to accept the culture of the whites. Maintenance of their native culture was reinforced by their occasional visits to the reservation. Indeed, they maintained dual cultures, retaining their native culture on the one hand and adopting the white culture on the other. Culturally, politically, economically, and structurally, the Choctaws in Riverville were semiautonomous.

The Choctaws in Riverville, to my belief, were peasants. There was no reason in my mind why they could not be called peasants. Traditionally, however, most of the American anthropologists who have specialized in peasantry have denied that there have been any peasants in the United States. It had been a sort of taboo to label any American community as peasant. They have come to believe that peasants must exist outside of the United States.

However, Arthur Raper was the only exception to this tradition. [40] After he studied two Georgia counties in the early 1930s, he was convinced that the mass tenants were becoming peasants rather than independent American farmers. He stated that:

The Black Belt plantation economy, whether regnant or declining prepares the land and the man for the emergence of a peasant rather than for the appearance of the traditional independent American farmer. Before the plantation structure crumbles, the owners dominate the economic and cultural life of the entire community, and a few of them may be relatively wealthy; but even then the majority of the plantation folk are subpeasants—no property, no self-direction, no hope of either. . . . Such are the beginnings of peasantry in the New World—the collapse of the Black Belt plantation system is a preface to American peasantry. [41]

Other authorities on peasants do not agree with the interpretation of Raper. Robert Redfield, for instance, mentioned in his lecture at The University of Stockholm in 1953 that: "Americans deny that any of themselves are or were peasant, in part, no doubt, because of their strong egalitarian and republican sentiments. But I think it is in truth the case that America did not develop a peasantry." [42] Foster has agreed saying "the long settled, skillful farmers of the pueblos in the American Southwest do not qualify as peasants, since their communities are (were) largely autonomous in political control and religious leadership." [43] Rather than use the word "peasant," he coined the phrase "a rural proletariat." I continue to have difficulty discerning the nuances of the difference between the two.

As a matter of fact, the Choctaws in Riverville were neither a tribal group nor urban dwellers. They were located in a niche between the tribal group and the white-dominated plural off-reservation milieu. Redfield himself once seemed to hint at the possibility of peasantry in America when he said, "It is curious that among all the Americans, the rural Negroes of the Old South came closest, in my opinion, to constituting a peasantry."[44] I have wondered why American anthropologists have been so reluctant to refer to any group of Americans as peasants, although they would never hesitate to employ the label outside the United States.

I categorized the characteristics of the Choctaws in Riverville as peasants in a paper presented at the ninth annual meeting of the Southern Anthropological Society.[45] By and large, my paper received a very cold reception that day. I drew the most questions and discussion in that session because it did not coincide with the expectations of the American anthropologists. It was enough for me to understand why the public of Georgia became so angry over Raper's use of the word "peasant" instead of using tenant or sharecropper in his book of *Preface to Peasantry*.[46]

Very often, I have been told that most Western anthropologists are proud of their being liberal in their values and masters of their ethnocentrism. Yet I learned that their capacity for tolerance of the strange notions of an outsider was far from limitless. Consequently, I agree with the observation made by Francis Hsu, a senior Asian anthropologist, when he said that "White anthropologists find it most intolerable to accept theories about their White American culture by non-White anthropologists, especially if the theories contradict the ones White anthropologists have already held dear."[47] Had I presented ethnographic information only in the role of fact-gatherer, without any attempt to theorize my data, I might have been received better.[48] Even in this limited role, Hsu remained skeptical by saying that: "Even in the role of fact gatherers, White anthropologists would like non-Whites to confine themselves to their own native non-White cultures, and not to poke into the White preserves where the White anthropologists were born, live, work, and raise their children."[49] He frankly expressed his fears about such high-mindedness:

We now come to the most important question. All right, I can imagine some of my White colleagues saying, you have dug up some convincing evidence that we Whites have not bothered with what you non-Whites have had to offer intellectually to our profession, but have we not done very well so far? Have we not gathered a great amount of data and built up an impressive body of theories about this and other societies? Let's face it and, mind you, I am not at all personally prejudiced, but we have gone our own way simply because you non-Whites have little or nothing of significance to offer.[50]

He further warned against prejudice in the intellectual world, not in terms of employment and educational opportunities but in the approaches of nonwestern schools:

In spite of its cross-cultural protestations, American anthropology will become White American anthropology unless our fraternity consciously takes a more open-minded approach to other competing assumptions—rooted in other cultures—about man and what makes him run. There is a world of difference between a truly cross-cultural science of man and a White-centered science of man with cross-cultural decorations.[51]

4

Going to Hilltown, Mississippi

In May 1974, on behalf of the Choctaw tribal government, my friend, John H. Peterson, Jr., phoned me to inquire about my availability as field director for a social, economic, and demographic study to be conducted on the Mississippi Band of Choctaw Indians. By this time, he was no longer the chief planner because his sabbatical term had expired, and he had returned to Mississippi State University to resume his duty as the department head. Yet he remained in very close association with the tribal government.

By his recommendation, he said, the tribal government was anxious to have me conduct the study and admitted that he was personally interested in seeing how the Choctaws would respond to an Asian anthropologist as an interesting study in itself for anthropological methodology. I accepted the post.

I immediately telephoned Bailey in Georgia to inform him of the offer. To my amusement, he already knew about it because he had been consulted during a check of my credentials. This reminded me that Americans like to use telephones. The Choctaw Indians were not exceptions. I had learned also that credit was the most important asset in American society, especially for a foreigner. Apparently, tribal officials had liked my former experiences. Besides my field experiences in South Georgia and West Tennessee, I had supervised data collection and processing for a section at the Center for Research in Social Change at Emory University as part of an OEO evaluation project while writing my master's thesis. There was no way of knowing whether or not my identity as an Asian anthropologist was a contributing factor in my selection for the post of field director, but I believe it was.

In addition to my personal qualifications, the project called for an anthropologist who was in some way related to two previous studies of the Mississippi Choctaws conducted in 1962 by Bailey and in 1968 by Peterson. As a student of Bailey, a personal friend of Peterson, and a researcher among the Riverville Choctaws, I seemed to meet the criterion adequately. Both previous studies had compiled the socioeconomic and demographic characteristics of the Choctaws. The 1968 survey had been warranted due to changes in the Choctaw society. The new 1974 survey was to obtain information regarding the Choctaw work force as well as to provide a data bank about each household for the tribal government and its service agencies.

Although I was experienced in working with whites, I felt a degree of uncertainty about the reactions of the whites of Hilltown (the nearest town to the reservation) to the project. The whites in Hilltown were reputed to be ultraconservative. Since the Bureau of Indian Affairs (BIA) Choctaw Agency is located in Hilltown, I would frequently associate with them.

If they thought of me as a Choctaw, I could expect poor treatment. I had been told they treated the Choctaw Indians badly. The Choctaws in Riverville had told me that the racial segregation applied to Indians in Hilltown was worse than that in West Tennessee. One of them had said, "When in Riverville, I could go into any barbershop and get my hair cut. But, down there I couldn't go in a barbershop. And we couldn't go in some restaurants, either." Even if I were identified as an Asian, I was told that I would not be received much better because the whites of the region were familiar with Orientals, mainly Chinese.

A short distance across the state in the Delta area, there were more than 1,200 Chinese.[1] Until they made economic and social achievements recently, those Chinese were classed with blacks in Mississippi. They had come into the state in 1869 and 1870, at a time when planters were recruiting agricultural labor, and had entered the social system at the bottom as sharecroppers. "Partly for this reason, White Mississippi considered them to be of roughly Negro status and barred them from white schools, organizations, and other social interaction."[2] Thus I had no reason to expect the sympathetic treatment I had received in Pinetown, Georgia.

During the 1973 Choctaw fair when I visited Hilltown, I had found an opportunity for assessing the responses of some Mississippi whites to an

Asian. While on a bus to Nanih Waiya Mound[3] three white ladies sitting behind me were talking loudly and having a good time. As their joking and teasing seemed to run out, one of them inquired about my residence. She did not ask the question very seriously. So I answered in a similar vein that I was a Choctaw from West Tennessee. "Are you kiddin'?" she asked. I insisted I was not. She moved up to sit beside me wanting to talk some more. The other two listened intently to our conversation. She could not believe I was a Choctaw Indian. "Don't you think he is an Oriental?" she asked her friends. Both replied they could not tell. My accent did not serve as a criterion, because many Choctaws also had thick accents. She continued to pester me until I finally admitted I was an Asian.

Considering her certainty as to my origin, I thought she must have traveled in some Oriental countries. Instead, she had grown up in a village near the Chinese population in the Delta region of Mississippi and was familiar with Orientals. She was a secretary at a university in Mississippi. Ironically, the other two ladies were anthropologists at the same university, and while they could not discern differences between Choctaws and Orientals, the secretary could. The secretary did not mention having any special feelings about Orientals, nor did she give any special treatment to the Oriental sitting beside her. I realized that if most of the whites in Hilltown and its vicinity treated me as the secretary had, then I might not have the particular advantage in Hilltown that I had had in Pinetown.

As the time for beginning the study drew near, I faced a practical problem. How could I recruit enough trained research assistants? The university in which I was teaching did not have a graduate program in either anthropology or sociology. It was too late to acquire graduate students from other institutions. The schools on the semester system had already begun their summer vacations. I could do nothing but recruit them from my classes.

A few students expressed interest in going to the reservation, not only because their services would be reasonably compensated but because they were curious about the native Americans as well. All in all, they were very sympathetic toward the Indians. Interestingly, however, no black students showed an interest although there were a number of black students in my classes. When I asked several black students personally, they simply said that they were not interested in the Indians. They had no sympathetic understanding of the Indians. Although none had ever observed the lives of American Indians on reservations, they felt certain that the Indians had been treated a lot better than themselves.

Finally, I was able to recruit twelve students, six male students and six female students. I had not intended to balance the sexes. However, it turned out to be ideal. If the research assistants had all been males, they would have had trouble obtaining information on visits to many Choctaw homes during the day because of the common absence of the working Choctaw males. If unnecessary suspicion had been aroused, the project might have been aborted. Also, I would not have been comfortable sending my female assistants to Choctaw homes where females were absent. I set up three crews with two males and two females in each. Also, each crew had at least two cars. This arrangement allowed the maximum flexibility for the overall conduct of the project.

The remaining problem was the basic training for the assistants. None had any previous experience working in research activities. They were unfamiliar with different ethnic groups. Most of them came from small towns in West Tennessee, so their experiences with other cultures had been extremely limited. A couple of weeks prior to going to the reservation, all of the selected assistants got together for a brief orientation. One of them brought up the fact that the town had a reputation of "red-neckishness" and mentioned the incident of the slaying of three civil rights workers there in 1964 who were buried in a pond bank with a bulldozer. Some were afraid the whites would still have particular notions about college students.

The description of Hilltown made by the student had its foundation. Indeed, the town had maintained its bad reputation for quite some time. Peterson has described the area this way:

National attention has been directed toward the sand clay hills only twice within the past one hundred years. First in 1878, the murder of members of the Chisolm family during Reconstruction resulted in one of the counties in the area becoming widely known as "Bloody" Kemper. . . . As recently as 1968, a national news magazine chose a third county in the sand clay hills as an example of backwardness and refusal to change in light of recent Supreme Court decisions regarding segregation. Even Mississippians, both Negro and White, from other regions of the state held the impression that the sand clay hills region is "rough" and "backward."[4]

When I addressed the students' fears, I knew they must be able to deal with the residents or not go at all, and so I told them not to hesitate in withdrawing if the prospects appeared too frightening. I then added that I felt the town was not greatly different from other towns across the nation. Almost any town might have a few isolated instances of violence. In big cities, there would be even more. Needless to say, my remarks were not sufficient to alleviate all their anxieties. Eventually, however, only one male dropped out and had to be replaced.

Their image of Hilltown deterred their mental readiness for moving into the white-dominated Mississippi town. Because of this, when I went to the reservation to discuss strategy with the officials of the tribal government, I asked whether it would be possible for my students to live on the reservation. If the students could stay on the reservation with the Indians, they would feel safer. Besides, it would also provide more opportunities to contact the Choctaws. The tribal planner in charge of the project assured me that it could be easily arranged. He suggested the dormitory of the Choctaw Central High School, located near the tribal office building. I was shown the inside of the dormitory and was very pleased with its excellent condition. All of my students were pleased to know they would be staying on the reservation with the Choctaw Indians rather than in Hilltown with the whites.

The questions from the students were never-ending. They expected me to answer everything categorically. That was rather natural. Since it was to be their first experience in an alien culture with alien people, they wanted to know how to prepare and how they should behave after getting there. They were asking basic questions about the field techniques of anthropological field work. I told them frankly there are few specific rules or techniques for successful field work. They were dissatisfied with the nature of my answer as I had been when I made similar inquiries of my teacher when starting my first field work. As a result, some students were skeptical about my credentials for anthropological field work. One asked me to invite a specialist who had more specific knowledge of field work. Someone even suggested we invite a historian who knew something about the Choctaw Indians to give a talk to the group. I did little but be patient. The techniques to be used would be dependent upon an individual's perception; some would adjust well in given circumstances and develop skill very quickly, while others would be unable to approach the natives at all. I related to my students a very ambiguous principle, which I had learned through my previous field work: a human relationship is reciprocal, regardless of how primitive, articulate, or civilized the people; if you behave correctly, the natives will respond in kind. Even a dog will be nice to you as long as you treat it properly.

The most sensitive questions came from the female students, such as how they should maintain their appearance. Could they wear jeans? How should they wear their hair? The questions were detailed, delicate, but certainly realistic. I then knew why so many female anthropologists have been very successful in carrying their field work into various exotic societies and cultures. I knew about problems with dress in the field from experience, as I have described already in an earlier chapter. Yet, it had never occurred to me to be concerned about the mode of female dress for an Indian reservation. It was totally alien for me to think about the role of females in the field. Furthermore, I was very unfamiliar with American female clothing and makeup, although I had lived in America for ten years. In all honesty, I did not have answers. I merely advised them to avoid any type of clothing which might draw too much attention to themselves.

In regard to this matter, Pelto has shown some of the delicate problems the female field worker must concern herself with:

Sometimes the simple practice of wearing fairly visible lipstick is enough to disassociate oneself from undesirable roles, such as that of missionary lady. It is important to keep in mind relationships between habits of dress and signaling of sexual attitudes. Sometimes wearing lipstick is, in itself, considered provocative; slacks and shorts are not appropriate attire in many areas of the world (though they are perfectly acceptable in others).[5]

Laura Nader has described her experiences relating to her hair style during field work saying that:

The women constantly badgered me to grow my hair, to change my hair, to change my clothes. By experimenting I finally discovered that the best reply was to tell them that were they to visit my home country dressed as they were with such long pigtails they would be ridiculed. . . . I capitalized on their indecision as to how to categorize me and gained the greatest freedom of movement among both men and women.[6]

At last, the female students of mine and I agreed to avoid any particular elements which might symbolize locally disliked types of white college students. At the same time, the problem of hair style and clothes of the male students was not as simple as I had at first suspected. Some had hair the same length as that of the female students. Some of them had long beards. They began to raise questions along with the female students. If they cut their hair very short, their necks would tan and they would appear the stereotyped image of the redneck, which symbolized the most disliked type of person among the Choctaw Indians. Yet, if they maintained their long hair, they would meet the disapproval of the local whites, because of the stereotyped image of the hippies, radicals, and college activists. The slain victims in 1964 had been college youths. I did not want my students to bring back forgotten memories of college activists.

Nevertheless, I did not give specific suggestions one way or the other. They all trimmed their hair and beards to more moderate lengths, however. I was very pleased by their willingness to adapt to the needs of the field work, and became more so when I heard the story of a white planner for the tribe. When he first came to Hilltown in 1971, he had been stopped by a local policeman because he had long hair. The policeman gave him a ticket and took his driver's license away from him.

On June 17, 1974, a very humid morning, our team began an eight-car caravan toward east central Mississippi. When we stopped at Mississippi State University near Starkville, it was already late afternoon. I wanted my students to meet Peterson, who had now returned as department head at Mississippi State University, and for him to give them a brief orientation about what to expect from both whites and Choctaws. Peterson was obviously disturbed, and I feared he had news for us. Without telling me anything, he suggested that I use his phone to call the tribal planner. The white planner told me the plan for our stay on the reservation had been rejected by the Choctaw Agency and the Choctaw School Board. We would have to stay in a local motel in Hilltown. We all shared Peterson's glumness. My students were faced with practical problems. They simply had not brought enough money to cover the expenses of staying in a motel and eating every meal in a restaurant. As for myself, how could I prevent friction from occurring between my students and the Hilltowners if we stayed in the town?

During the telephone conversation with the planner, he said that the rejection was motivated by long-standing antagonism between two bureaucratic systems, the Choctaw Agency, the local office of the BIA of the U.S. Department of the Interior, and the Indians' self-governing body. I had been told previously that activities of the two organizations lacked coordination, and I figured this must be another example in support of that opinion. Without the approval of the school board and the Choctaw Agency, I had wondered how the tribal government planner could make such a strong commitment to me. The position of the white planner was designed as the tribal government's middleman for the project. I now realized his capacity was limited.

We moved into the motel temporarily with a maximum number in each room. Although I knew he could not do anything about it, I continued to badger the planner about living up to his earlier commitment. As a result, he told me of a number of policies for the Indians on the reservation that have suffered from the dual bureaucratic systems. He felt the inefficiency was a primary source of discontent among young, educated Indians.

Most of the students were fairly conscious of our position in the town, but they were restlessly moving in and out of the motel room and the office until the late evening. Many of the Hilltowners watched us suspiciously, but the suspicion, curiosity, and anxiety were really mutual. One evening, as some students were leaving, one said, "We're going to see the rednecks instead of being the show." I shouted after them, "Knock it off! Nowadays, everyone has long hair covering their rednecks! You can't see any rednecks around here!"

After a week at the motel, I knew that I had to arrange for new living quarters because the students were already running out of money. Also, gossip and rumors were starting, and I wanted no conflict with local whites. I was informed that we had already drawn the attention of local state troopers. They had issued traffic violation tickets to some of my students. It was a well-known tactic commonly used against civil rights workers in the 1960s. I brought the students' attention to the matter and asked them to conform carefully to the traffic regulations of the town.

Actually, I usually drove more carelessly than my students, but I did not receive a ticket. Once, I stopped my car at a parking meter and spent too much time inside a store. When I returned, I found a green ticket stuck to my car windshield. I thought I had finally gotten mine. It read, "Welcome visitor to our growing city. Our city extends to you a cordial welcome, and hopes you will return often—Police Department." The other side read, "This card entitles you to park your car as long as you please. Never mind the time limit (but please be reasonable)."

Because of this green welcome note, I began to reassess the image of the Hilltown policemen. I wondered if my students and I were too preoccupied with the tragedy of the slaying of the three civil rights workers in 1964. It had been ten years. That was long enough to bring about a lot of changes in Hilltown. I suspected that my students might have deserved the tickets. I was not aware of further instances of ticketing.

In any event, I realized, the role of my students needed to be known to the public. This might eliminate unnecessary rumors and suspicion as to our mission. And I prepared a big name tag that was easily visible for each student. It had the name, university affiliation, and job assignment, indicating "research assistant for the Choctaw Manpower Survey." I was hoping that would help clarify our position. At the same time, I reminded the students that this project would provide the basic data for recruiting some industries. I knew the natives would probably be responsive to that idea. However, there was no way of knowing how much this would contribute to a change of our image.

As our housing problem remained unresolved and our situation was not improving, I was becoming desperate and decided to take action. And so I just walked into the office of the tribal chairman and explained the whole matter without going through the middleman. I intended to cut the bureaucratic red tape.

The chairman had not been told anything about our housing situation, nor had he been informed of our hardships. He phoned the superintendent of the Choctaw Agency. The superintendent loaned us a new house trailer which he sent to the reservation and had set up for us. The tribal government provided an empty house. In this way, it took only a few hours to straighten out our housing problems. I assigned the six females to the new trailer and the six males to the house. The planner had deceived me all along. There were no major bureaucratic complexities between the Choctaw Agency and the tribal government. Instead, only the planner was on poor terms with the agency. (The planner had left the reservation prior to the completion of our project for a personal reason.)

I successfully moved my students to the reservation. However, our problems did not end with the moving. Some Choctaw officials expressed concern about our male students being on the reservation. Their worry was that my students would have affairs with the Choctaw girls. At the same time, I was worrying about my female students. The planner expressed both concerns. Some officials seemed to expect me to patrol both living quarters at night. As a matter of fact, the planner did not want me to leave town on weekends to visit my family. I jokingly told them not to worry because I had brought an equal number of males and females. But I worried. I was staying at a motel in town, which was about ten miles away from the reservation. I did not feel comfortable having the responsibility for twelve students. In a sense, it was worse than conducting field work alone.

Given my new station, I realized my field work in Pinetown had been easier to handle, because I had only been responsible for myself. In Pinetown, I could usually get sympathetic assistance from the natives who knew I was a foreigner in need of help. But having twelve of my students in my charge, I no longer could get such sympathetic assistance. I was being subjected to a test of my leadership. My ability to control my students was doubted, particularly by the planner. Virtually everyone directly or indirectly involved with the project maintained the wait-and-see attitude of an onlooker. Simultaneously, however, my students seemed to sense this pattern. Hence in order to eliminate such attitudes, my students showed a great deal of respect for me and worked harder than I had expected. Some worked late into the evening averaging sixteen hours a day. If I had been a native white American professor, they might not have worked as hard as they did for me. They seldom created any problem requiring my extra time and energy.

I was gratified with the excellent job my students were performing. However, I was obliged to pay attention to the Choctaw college students who were assigned to serve as interpreters and guides for my students. Their roles were essential to the project, because they knew the Indian communities and there were quite a few Choctaw households that contained no English-speaking persons. But for some of them, their jobs were just a means of making some spending money during summer vacation. For me, however, they were potentially key informants for the project.

After they joined our team, they were a source of abiding frustration because they did not show any enthusiasm at all. It was my first experience as supervisor of American Indians. I did not know what would reinforce their work or how I could cheer them up. They were supposed to come to my office every morning at eight o'clock with my students, then I could assign them to a certain job for the day. None showed up on time. Later, usually after the students had already gone to the field without them, two or three would arrive and sit quietly with nothing to do. Even then, whenever I asked them to identify a certain Choctaw individual, their answer was commonly "I don't know 'im." I felt the rumblings of dissension and sabotage, but I did not know what I could do about it.

My students complained about this seeming indifference of the Choctaw students. I had assigned certain Choctaw students to each crew, and so when they did not come or came late, it disturbed the schedule of my students. Soon, whenever one of us arrived late, he would be asked if he were operating on "Choctaw time."

One of my students complained to a white official in charge of the Choctaw students' payroll. The white man came by my office and asked me to report their time sheets for their pay checks. He specifically asked me whether they were idle while on their jobs. If they were, he said he could do something about it. He was expecting me to complain. Instead, I told him that everything was just fine. They were doing their best and deserved to be paid in full. I knew he would tell them everything I said. I had deduced that if I were the source of any negative impression of them, I would never get their cooperation.

By this time, I had been informed that the Choctaw students were complaining as to why they could not be the research assistants instead of interpreters and why the white college students had received the positions instead of them. It was rumored that my students were being paid extraordinary amounts for their roles. The Choctaw students realized that if they served as the research assistants, the money for the project would stay on the reservation. Also, there would be no need for interpreters. They were confident that they could perform the dual roles. One Choctaw student criticized the planner about this matter in my presence. The reason their desire could not be implemented was the ethics involved in having local people ask personal questions of local people with whom they live throughout the year.

Although it was not true that my students were paid large sums, the rumor spread around the reservation and to the Choctaw Agency in Hilltown. Some potentially good informants flatly refused to answer our inquiries saying something like, "Since you're paid so well, you should find that out for yourself. If I can answer the question, I should be paid for it." This sort of answer came mainly from white clerical workers in the various agencies.

My job seemed to be getting more difficult and tedious than in the first stage. I felt a little public relations would help. I instructed my students to get involved in community activities and continue acquaintances with the Choctaw youths. I told them that the important thing was to let people know that we were not there just to make money. We had also come to share and exchange our cultures on the basis of mutual respect. As they made many acquaintances, often Choctaw youths would visit their living quarters. In fact, sometimes, too many came or they stayed so late that resting hours were disrupted. Despite our sincere efforts to get along harmoniously with the Choctaws and the other whites on the reservation, the overall response was indignant stand-offishness.

One small incident served as impetus for a major breakthrough in our relations with Choctaws and white BIA and tribal employees. At seven o'clock one evening, all of the students were due to be in the office of Social Services of the Choctaw Agency, in order to obtain the tribal roll numbers of some of our Choctaw respondents from files there. I had made arrangements for us to use the facilities during evening hours to prevent our being underfoot throughout the working day. Because the files contained confidential information on each client, we had to work under supervision. Each evening, the director arrived with one or two employees, usually one white and one Choctaw, who aided us in obtaining the needed information. That particular evening, the employees and director arrived promptly, but only a couple of students were on time. I was greatly embarrassed and became even more so as over half of the students came about an hour late. I decided to make the best of a bad situation. I should reproach my students to prevent internalization of poor work habits. Also, I wanted to take advantage of the presence of the white and the Choctaw employees to spread word of my authority and create an aura of sympathy for my students. Thus I called my students together and began my "sermon," using some strong language:

Some of you have used the term, "Choctaw time," complaining that the Choctaw students come in late every morning. Now, you come in an hour later than when I instructed you to come. Is this "white middle-class time" then? Is this your attitude toward American Indians, criticizing them while doing the same? When you become the leaders of this country in the future, as eventually you will, with that kind of attitude, I'll feel sorry for you and myself as one of your teachers. Some of the Choctaw students might do this job better than some of you. But I can't put them to work as research assistants because they would be put in a precarious position and could not obtain access to these confidential files because of their personal knowledge of the people involved. I brought you down here, not because you were better qualified than the Choctaw students, but because you were a third party.

Some of the students knew they had become scapegoats that evening, but most received my chiding at face value. Thereafter, my students showed up promptly and worked even harder than previously. Some worked until eleven o'clock at night, yet reported at eight o'clock the next morning. Simultaneously, the students became involved in the cultural affairs of the Choctaws. Several advised some Choctaw Central High School students about techniques in acting, makeup, and set design in preparation for a play to be held at the annual Choctaw fair.

Meanwhile, my reprimand of the students had circulated on the reservation and throughout the BIA offices. As the story circulated, it established that I was not a helpless foreign professor who could not control his students. It also eliminated the resentment of the Choctaw students. They began to show up early in the morning. Some came earlier than my students. They offered their sincere cooperation. If they did not know certain Choctaws, they attempted to identify them by asking other Choctaws whom they felt would know. Some Choctaws began to call me "Kung Fu" named after the television show, the main character of which was a humble Oriental wandering around the nation to help the underdogs in some mysterious ways. The diligence of my students coupled with the cooperation of the Choctaw students resulted in completion of the schedule of virtually all field work long before anyone had thought possible.

In the same period, the attitudes of onlookers had reversed. Several white employees on the reservation criticized me for overworking my students. They too referred to me as Kung Fu in the presence of my students because of my hardline handling of my students. They perceived me as a diligent little Oriental who was unbearably demanding of his students. That attitude was definitely preferable to the earlier rumors that my students were lazy and overpaid. I never slackened my watchfulness, however, because I knew a simple mistake could disturb the good rapport we had so painstakingly gained.

The project taught me a very important lesson in field work: that a single event could alter people's attitudes drastically. Another such occasion occurred when I was having a working lunch with some students. As is my custom, I felt obliged to take all the tabs. The waitress added them and I paid her. The amount had seemed too low, so I later calculated the sum myself. She had undercut the total some five dollars. I returned to the restaurant and paid the rest. Until then, no one had noticed the discrepancy. The waitress was surprised by my honesty. She often repeated the story to customers and seemed to tell everyone she knew. Soon, I was known as an honest Oriental as well as a diligent one.

Because of its notoriety, I wanted to make a special effort to view Hilltown only on the basis of first-hand contact. In order to do this, I maintained my residence in Hilltown during the field work on the reservation. For the first week, I stayed in an inexpensive motel with my students. When they moved to the reservation, I moved into a moderately priced one, located at the edge of Hilltown. It was a nice, clean, and quiet place.

Although I was interacting with the townspeople everyday, I realized that the longer I stayed in the town, the harder I found it to delineate the characteristics of Hilltown. My overall assessment on the nature of Hilltown was one of ambivalence: the town was not as bad as it had been depicted, yet it was certainly not as tolerant as most other southern towns, particularly in its racial perspectives toward the local blacks and Choctaws.

Personally, I could not have expected any better hospitality. My earlier speculation that I would be treated differently than I had in the other parts of the South because of the Chinese population in the Mississippi Delta area was proven untrue. Numerous occurrences indicated to me that Hilltowners were the same as the southern gentlemen and ladies who had been warm and friendly to me in Pinetown.

As indicated already, there was the parking meter incident in which I received a cordial welcome note instead of getting a penalty. When the motel restaurant closed for the Fourth of July holiday, the motel owner called me personally and made special arrangements for me. The custodian of the motel knew that I worked late in my room in the evening and brought me an extra table for my writing. Whenever I lunched in a certain small café, the owner would companionably come, sit, and talk with me. When I dropped by the restaurant between meals, he would serve me free cups of coffee. In a sense, Hilltowners were more receptive toward me than the Pinetowners in South Georgia and Toptowners in West Tennessee. If I had not been alerted about Hilltown's reputation, I would have felt comfortable from the beginning.

However, I realized the white Hilltowners were not friendly to everyone, particularly to the nonwhites. I was an exception. For instance, the town's movie theater segregated seating and admission fees by the color line. The blacks and the Choctaws were charged less than the whites but had to sit in the balcony. Once, several of my students went to the theater and asked to be seated in the balcony. They were not being activists; they had simply thought it would be economical. When they were not allowed to do so, they left. One angered student asked me to see how I would be treated racially at the theater. It would have been an interesting experiment, but it would have brought about their embarrassment as well. Such embarrassment might have had unpredictable effects. I thought I should avoid such temptation and continue to enjoy my unique status.

Segregation could also be seen in restaurants. Most, including the one affiliated with the motel, were open to anyone. Probably owing to discomforting social pressure, few blacks or Choctaws frequented them, however. But one restaurant barred nonwhites.

One day, I roamed the six Choctaw communities composing the reservation with a Choctaw guide to see my assistants in action. At dinnertime, I asked the Choctaw student if he knew a good eating place. He took me to a small restaurant in town but did not want to go inside. I thought he did not have money to pay for his meal and so I told him I would pay for it. Finally, he told me his reluctance was not a matter of money, but was owing to a taboo about allowing blacks or Choctaws in that place. I was embarrassed and found myself with nothing to say. He grinned crookedly trying not to show emotion. Instead of going into the restaurant, we drove back to the reservation. I had lost my appetite.

After returning to the reservation that day, I stood in the yard of the tribal office building under the blazing sun of that Mississippi summer. My mind was preoccupied by the facial expression of the Choctaw student. I could not forget the moment when he was wondering whether he should tell me or not. It was beyond my comprehension as to why those meek Choctaws were barred from a public place. I became very skeptical about my role as an anthropologist and what I was doing on the reservation for the Choctaws. I found myself to be a helpless onlooker.

At that moment, a quite ludicrous incident occurred which did nothing to increase my self-confidence or lessen my skepticism. An old man sauntered up and said, "You're a doctor, aren't you?" I told him I was. "Please, don't refuse what I'd like to ask," he pleaded. I assured him I would not. He then mentioned having back trouble and a problem of blood in his urine. He wanted to know if the latter was related to his kidney. I told him that I knew nothing about it. He complained, "You see, you doctors always say you don't know nothing for sure 'til you're sure you'll get paid." Since most of the employees of the tribal government and my students addressed me as "doctor," he thought I was a physician. I explained that I was not a physician. He could not understand that anyone other than medical doctors could be addressed as such. Then, several Choctaw children behind him asked me to demonstrate my karate skill. I told them I knew nothing about it. The disappointed old Choctaw sullenly complained, "What do you know, then?" I could not even answer that simple but fundamental question.

The old man's words led me to some introspection. I became increasingly skeptical about the worth of my previous training in anthropology for field work. In the field, personal skill and adaptability were constantly demanded in order to adjust to the delicate field situations. For instance, I could not recall any lecture or literature that had taught me how to handle the white employees of Indian reservations. Occasionally, I found myself in an awkward position. The white employees wanted to exercise authority over me. They had a common belief that they knew the Choctaw Indians better than I. Hence they would attempt to become involved in almost every activity, even if it was a technical area of the field work. I wanted to avoid any direct clash with them, yet I could not be under their control.

For instance, the differences in opinion between the white planner and myself began when I was preparing the questionnaire. The project's proposal required the data-gathering of certain demographic characteristics which necessitated door-to-door interviews of each Choctaw household. This meant that my twelve research assistants and the eight Choctaw interpreters must interview approximately eight hundred households scattered around seven large Choctaw communities. Obviously, the project would be a time-consuming job and the proposal's timetable was such that the first stage of the field work had to be completed during the summer. I intended to shorten the questionnaire covering the contents of the proposal and little else. However, the planner wanted to please everyone and tried to include their wishes in the questionnaire. Most such items were not related to the proposed project. I explained to him many times that one questionnaire could not ask for and contain all information one wishes to have, but it did not make sense to him. When the planner could not explain to me why certain items should be included, he would say the tribal government had demanded it. This frustrated me, but I could do nothing except compromise. One item that I was unable to strike was the request for tribal roll numbers. The tribal roll numbers had nothing to do with a socioeconomic and demographic study. Later, that one item became our greatest source of frustration because no Choctaw knew his number and most did not know there was such a number. As already mentioned, we eventually had to get these numbers from files.

Needless anxiety was created again when we sought to get the questionnaire approved by an official of the funding agency. My research assistants and I were already using the questionnaire not knowing whether our work would be acceptable. Meanwhile, the planner was supposed to have sent the final version of the questionnaire to the funding agency. After a reasonable waiting period, we contacted the official to inquire about our status, but he told us he had not received the questionnaire. He also said he was leaving in a few days for an extended vacation. So, if we wanted approval, we needed to get it to him quickly. The planner insisted that he had sent the questionnaire. I suggested that he send another copy by airmail or special delivery. He answered that he would not. He did not manifest it, but his ambivalence led me to believe that he did not see any need to hurry. Furthermore, he was saying inadvertently that no matter how I hustled, I could not finish the survey portion before my students went back to school for fall quarter. If I could, it would be a miracle.

Ironically, the difficulty in doing field work on the reservation was not in dealing with the Indians, but rather such incidents as just mentioned that were the doings of the white employees. Indeed, the whites on the reservation considered themselves as the authorities who really understood the Indians because of their lengthy service. They were sympathetic and believed themselves to be dedicated to the Indians. On many occasions they manifested to me their skepticism regarding what anthropologists know about, have done for, and can do for the Indians.

Traditionally, the missionary has not been an exception in evaluating the roles of anthropologists negatively. And one missionary sent to the reservation by a small theological seminary in Mississippi gave me a long sermon in the presence of several Choctaws in his trailer home saying that anthropologists had failed to "civilize" the Indians. He stated that the roles of the anthropologists were dysfunctional for the civilization of the native Americans on the reservation. Finally, he concluded aloud that anthropology was an anti-Christian discipline. I did not know how to react to that paradoxical statement. The Choctaws who were present had never concerned themselves about understanding anthropology until the missionary began interpreting the discipline using his frame of reference. It appeared that he had managed, in his few words, to bring a negative image of anthropology to the Indians. I realized that it would be very difficult for me to change those beliefs. In such cases, I listened quietly to whatever was said.

Among the Choctaws, I usually maintained myself in a low-key position and remained as an humble Oriental. Their attitudes toward me emerged gradually. They seemed not to stereotype me as an anthropologist. I often behaved like a total stranger to American ways and the ways of the Choctaws as well. Sometimes, I asked for their assistance even if it was not necessary for a job. They realized that I was not the kind of anthropologist who would overrun the authority of tribal officials. They did not think of me as the kind of person who could do things alone. They knew I needed their help and began offering their assistance. One who was critical of me during the preliminary stage of the project came to me and volunteered his help. I realized that I was being viewed with pity, but I thought that was better than having confrontations with them.

Considering my personal success in contacts with individual Choctaws prior to the project, I thought the project would be accepted also. My conviction became concrete when I considered that the project was not initiated by me but by their own tribal government, and further that the purpose of the project was not academic but rather that the data was to be used as a means of improving the living conditions of the Indians through tribal planning.

However, soon after coming to Mississippi, I realized that I had been too optimistic. Often, I was discouraged to find that Choctaw community leaders only passively supported the project. But I felt this lethargy might have occurred because they were unaware that the study had been planned to collect information for industrial development to employ Choctaws and for other planning projects beneficial to the Indians. I had asked the planner to send a memorandum from the tribal council chairman to community leaders explaining the details of the project and asking their full support. Later I found out the planner had not sent the memorandum before we started to work on the project. Indeed, he had not done it at all. I again asked him to do so, but it never materialized.

When I had realized the tribal government had not fully informed the Choctaws about the project, I started my own campaign to let them know the nature of the project, hoping for positive feedback. My students and I stressed that the project was planned and administered by the tribal government for the improvement of the Choctaws. Nevertheless, quite a few Choctaws expressed skepticism, wondering what they could possibly get out of it. If the white planner had sent the memorandum, much of this suspicion would have been eliminated. One Choctaw very cynically commented:

I came from the project rather than from the reservation. You know what I mean? You see, there are a lotta projects for the Indians. The money for the projects goes to someone else, not for the Indians. What did I get out of the projects? I might die in the projects without taking advantage from the damn projects. Even with the projects, we are still poor. Without the projects, we couldn't be much worse off. Projects and studies—hell, forget 'em.

For this Choctaw, it did not make any difference who initiated the project or what its purpose was. For him, Vine Deloria's outspoken Indian manifesto might look modest.[7]

A commonly more hostile group of Choctaws were the relatively younger, better-educated Choctaws. They sometimes directly challenged the contents of the questionnaire saying certain questions violated the civil rights of the Choctaws. One item of debate was, for instance, related to the degree of Indian blood one had, such as full blood, half blood, and so on. This question could indirectly seem to be in the interest of tracing possible illegitimacy rather than in protecting the tribe from false claims for tribal membership.

No matter what procedure had been used in constructing the questionnaire, from the professional point of view it was awkward. I was not satisfied with its final version. I regretted the compromises I made with my professionalism. One of my research assistants who was harassed by some Choctaw activists was told that they were threatening to prepare a legal suit against our crew and the tribal government. They were also angry with the Choctaw Agency because the agency had allowed us access to confidential files in order to get tribal roll numbers. In the end, there was no suit, but for a while I was worried. My concern was not whether they would file suit, but what the result of such litigation might be on future anthropological research at the reservation.

Knowing that my affiliation with the tribal government proved a disadvantage in my relationship with the Choctaws who were critical of it, I attempted to make the most of being an Asian, which had been very helpful in my contacts with the Choctaws in Riverville, Tennessee. I tried this approach when I was invited to speak at a meeting of the tribal council:

As you can see me, I'm an Oriental who looks very similar to the American Indians. If I say I'm a Chickasaw, you wouldn't know the difference. I'm an anthropologist, but my background is a unique one of being a yellow. You can't find many yellow or red anthropologists around. Hence, my interest in the Choctaws is unique. My interest in the Choctaw is the same kind as your interest in me and Orientals. My view of the Choctaw Indians may be a different one compared to the views of the others, because I have noticed many cultural similarities between your and my native society. For instance, yesterday evening I sat down in Joan's yard watching the smoke from a pile of leaves being used to keep the mosquitoes away. I became very nostalgic about it, because I can remember the same practice in Korean peasant villages. And, also, as I saw Joan's mother, she brought back memories of my grandmother whom I had forgotten while I have been living here in America. In some ways, I feel as if I am in my native village attending the meeting of the village elders. I feel I should speak Korean, illusion though it is, and you would understand the language. In any event, I hope this opportunity will allow me to understand Choctaw culture better and that my service for the project will be beneficial for the Choctaw people.

My brief speech before the councilmen was very well received. Indeed, the reception of many was as emotional as I had been when talking about my native culture and peoples. One councilman declared loudly, "Orientals're all right." Almost all of the councilmen came up to me and were very friendly. Some of them who had been in Korea for their military service after World War II or during the Korean conflict agreed with me that the culture of the Korean peasants was much the same as that of the Choctaws. They also admitted that when they saw the Korean peasants, they felt a closeness to them because they looked very similar to their own people.

Utilizing my personal appearance as an Oriental seemed to be a very efficient way to approach the Choctaw community leaders. Following the meeting with the councilmen, I was scheduled to visit a community, which is located nearly seventy miles away from the tribal office building. Owing to its location, not many Choctaws in the tribal office area knew about the Choctaws who lived in that community. The Choctaw students admitted they would be of little help. One councilman who worked in the tribal office voluntarily offered to guide me around the community. When I got there, the councilman from that community was waiting for my arrival, although he had not slept at all the previous night because of his night-shift job. He stayed with me all day helping to identify each household. Another councilman who went with me told me this was the first time he had ever seen the councilman show such enthusiasm in support of a research project.

In all honesty, there was no way of discerning whether my role-playing as an applied anthropologist and/or an Asian anthropologist on the Choctaw reservation was successful or not. However, there were many indications that it was. When I asked the white planner about a minor manipulation of the project schedule near the end of the project, he answered brightly, "This is your project and you are the director." When the survey portion was over ahead of schedule and the project was moving into the second phase at the end of summer, I had to send my students back home, except for the two most reliable students who were responsible for the second phase.

One evening, during this time, while I was sitting in a corner of the motel restaurant alone, the tribal chairman came by and patted my shoulder saying that everyone he had talked to thought I had done a good job. He asked me then whether there was any matter that I felt needed to be studied after the ongoing project was finished. He told me, "Frankly, I don't like some of the graduate students who come to the reservation and do their work for a thesis. It takes a lot of our time away and we don't get any advantage out of it. But, I'm ready for this sort of project any time because the Choctaws profit a great deal." His words reminded me of Eileen Maynard's recent article in which she referred to "a redefinition of the anthropologist's role":

It is apparent that it is no longer feasible to carry out research for research's sake or regard reservations as convenient laboratories for the study of an alien culture. Indians are reaching or have reached the point of satiation in regard to research, especially research without beneficial consequences. There are two possible alternative roles for the anthropologist on reservations. Ideally, applied research should be carried out at the request of the tribal government. Also, ideally, funds should be available for the development phase. This, of course, is an easier-said-than-done proposition, but there ought to be at least some assurance that the research is wanted and needed and that there is a strong possibility of the results being utilized or at least heeded. [8]

My role as field director in the project pleased me greatly for it seemed close to the ideal which Maynard has constructed.

Nevertheless, the role of the anthropologist on the reservation was not always bright and easy-going. For instance, it was not easy to convey the message to individual Indians that the study was initiated by the tribal government for the welfare of the Indians. Even if one did get across that message to the natives, one was not assured of a warm reception. In some instances, such affiliation with the tribal government would become disadvantageous because the natives would express their dissatisfaction with the policies of the tribal government through the research of the anthropologist. Whenever I faced such difficulties, I attempted to be seen as an Asian instead of an anthropologist.

There is a strong indication that the more educated and younger group of Choctaws are challenging the conventional leaders who are less educated, relatively older, and who developed their leadership abilities through the military services. It seems inevitable that the replacement of the conventional elite with those better-educated and more sophisticated younger Choctaws will come into being. I still wonder, if and when the transition takes place, how the new breed of Indians will treat anthropologists and what will be the roles of anthropologists. I hope that my fellow American anthropologists will still be able to go to the reservations for field work instead of going to the National Archives or to the libraries.

Epilogue: The South and Southern Hospitality

Since I am not a black whose ancestors were the slaves of white owners, I cannot understand the deeply rooted emotional feeling of blacks toward whites. And I am not a white who understands the position of whites in dealing with blacks in a racially plural society. Also, I may never be able to share the frustration and defeatist attitudes of the American Indians.

I have tried putting myself in the shoes of a member of each of these three racial groups, but I have not been successful in understanding them. The harder I have tried, the more confused I have become. When I listened to whites' criticisms of blacks, I felt their views about blacks were plausible. Yet, when I became acquainted with blacks, the whites' treatment of blacks appeared to be unfair. From the complaints of Indians about the white-dominated government, I drew the assumption that the whites were being deceptive. However, when I closely examined the programs designed by the government to improve the lives of the American Indians, the Indians appeared uninterested about overcoming their generations-old poverty. When I once heard an argument among some Indians and blacks about which group had been treated worse, I became further confused. Finally, I concluded that I could not fully understand each side of the story, because I was affiliated with no one group and could never be immersed in the attitudes of any particular group. Paradoxically, however, my neutral position facilitated my objective observation of each group. Each group was willing to present its side to me, because these people knew I did not represent any side.

At different times, each group has become too emotional in justifying its actions. Commonly, the white southerners receive the blame for the problems of all. Sometimes, of course, the white southerners do not deserve the blame and never all of it. But there has been a consistent pattern that the whites are allowed little chance to appeal this blame publicly. For instance, the racial bigotry expressed by some white southerners is definitely taboo on the national scene. This point of view has been overplayed, however, by the various media with the result that generalized negative attitudes have been applied to all white southerners. Usually, the white southerners remain quiet. It is my observation that so many allusions have been made to the real and supposed prejudices of southerners that they and their region have become objects of prejudice and discrimination as well. This treatment of the South has become so traditional that southerners no longer have any special feeling about it.

In cases of racial conflict in a small southern town, the national media is likely to generalize indirectly if not directly from the particular to the whole of the South. But if instances of racial strife occur in northern cities, the media are certain to specify the city and not generalize. As an example, the problems in 1974 and 1975 with school desegregation in Boston, Massachusetts, were reported by the national news media not as a school desegregation conflict in Massachusetts or even in Boston, but as a high school desegregation conflict in South Boston. If similar confrontation had occurred in southern cities, the media might have chosen to not be quite so generous with their specifications.[1] For too long the rest of the nation or at least the media pretended to believe that large-scale racial tension existed only in the South. This façade doubtlessly contributed to the ignoring of local race problems which has resulted in riots in black and other ethnic communities of northern cities and turmoil in Mexican-American communities in cities throughout the Southwest.

There has been a saying among white southerners, as Killian has noted, that, "Southerners love Negroes as individuals but dislike them as a group: Yankees love them as a group but hate them as individuals."[2] I can no longer accept that as true. There have been many indications that the South has undergone changes that have improved race relations. Regardless of its achievement, however, many of the national media still have not changed their attitudes toward their stories. This unfair treatment has existed at least since 1904 when Edgar Murphy indicated, "When our northern journalism discusses wrongs at the North or at the West, it criticizes the wrongs, but when it discusses wrongs at the South, it criticizes the South."[3] Because of this tendency, the South often appears in the national scene as the "dark, mysterious land of prejudice, poverty, and decadence."[4] Hence it has been ignored that the South also is progressive, heterogeneous, changing, and rapidly losing its regional distinctiveness.[5]

Indeed, the South changes and a New South is always emerging. Technology expands, the landscape is reshaped. Such changes are apparent in all the southern cities and much of the southern countryside. For instance, although I had lived in Atlanta for several years after 1965, I was quite unfamiliar with the downtown area when I visited there recently. It seemed to me that the city had grown twice in size since my arrival in America.

Often behavioral patterns of southerners who live in urban cities deviate from the traditional southern way of thinking—"its political conservatism, its aristocratic tradition, and its esteem for people and land rather than for technology."[6] However, for one to call the South "the last hope of America," as do a school of writers who cherish the South's gentility and stalwartness, is as unrealistic a view of the area as that held by nonsoutherners who have treated the South as the retarded child of the nation.

Regarding the pattern of racism in the South, Killian has made the interesting observation that "while White Americans in other regions practiced racism, however, only White southerners made of it an ideology. The South is still the only region in which open espousal of this ideology is a political asset, although some cities (Los Angeles, for example) are becoming more 'southern' in this respect."[7] Instead of discussing directly the validity of this statement made by Killian as to whether or not the white southerners made of racism an ideology, I would prefer to present my perspective on southern racism by describing my observation made in a small town in southwestern Georgia.

In 1965, while a dormitory resident at Emory, I was invited by my black suite-mate, Jim, to spend the Thanksgiving holidays with his family in Aville, Georgia, about 200 miles away from Atlanta. I at first declined his kind invitation because I was still in a stage of cultural shock, having come to America less than two months before. (Whenever invited to the home of any American family, I found that I would become exhausted, because I constantly had to pay attention to my behavior so as not to affront the host family.) His invitation was genuine. He was concerned about me because the entire school would be closed during the holidays. I told him the university would make some special arrangements for the foreign students who did not have anywhere to go. (Later, I found that this was not true.) Jim asked me if I was reluctant to visit a black family. I realized that if I did not go, no matter how I explained my discomfort with staying in Americans' homes, he would misunderstand me. Thus I was obliged to accept his invitation.

The living standard of Jim's family was lower than that of the community near Emory. But I was not surprised, particularly because such poverty was common in rural Korean peasant villages. The outdoor toilet was not foreign to me, because I used them extensively during my field work in the peasant villages in Korea. When I visited Jim's brother's house one evening, I realized the seven family members shared two rooms and only two beds. I got a headache smelling the strong odor of the two rooms, but I could stand it because I could feel their humanness toward me.

That visit was my first personal experience with the poverty of America. I had thought all Americans were wealthy, and this enabled America to give foreign aid to the poor countries of the world. However, I saw the same poverty I had seen in remote and isolated Korean rural villages. Interestingly, however, Jim's family and their neighbors showed sympathy to me, realizing that I came from a country which had been, and still is to a certain extent, a recipient of American foreign aid. As Americans, they were aware that they were donors of this foreign aid and, despite their poverty, assumed they were nevertheless among the wealthiest people in the world. Some showed me their telephone and television, assuming that I might never have seen those cultural items.

During my visit at Jim's home in Aville, I was told there was a Korean art instructor, John Wilson, teaching in a state college near there. He was a Korean War orphan who was adopted by white American parents in his early boyhood. I was very anxious to meet him. And so I plagued my suite-mate until he took me to Wilson's place. The house was located in a relatively wealthy white section of the town. I spoke to him in Korean, but he could not understand it. Also, he had no memories of Korea. He knew only that his adopted American parents had told him that he was born in Korea and had lost his parents during the Korean War. Excepting his physical appearance, he was no longer a Korean. Instead, he was a near perfect example of the stereotype of the American southerner.

I was first discouraged by not having a chance to use my native language. Yet, that was understandable. But then a real surprise came when our introduction was over. Wilson turned to Jim and said, "When ye called me on the phone, I didn't know ye were a colored boy. Ye know, ye shouldn't come in here!" Jim nodded and looked downcast. He asked Jim to leave immediately. "Ye jus' go back right now. I'll take this fellow to yer place later." I was very embarrassed since I had pestered my friend to arrange the meeting. I deeply regretted having insisted. Wilson's attitude was ludicrous in my view, for he also appeared to be a colored person if yellow is a color.

Jim politely accepted this admonition, did as he was bidden, and left me with Wilson. After my friend had left, Wilson warned me against close association with blacks. He said, "If ye hang around with Negroes, ye'll be treated jus' like one 'a them. But, as long as ye keep away from 'em, white folks around here will treat ya all right." According to his explanation, Orientals would be treated just like a white so long as they stayed away from blacks. The racial perspective of the adopted Korean orphan reverberated the words of the businessman in San Francisco, who had been schooled in the South. In any event, it was a saddening experience to witness the racial orientation of the Korean orphan.

Although I had heard about racism, feared it, and hesitated to come to the South because of it, until then I had no real knowledge of it. I knew Wilson's behavior was learned from whites, including his foster parents. But there was a special feeling for me because he was a native-born Korean. If he had grown up in Korea, he might not have learned racism because there were no other racial groups in Korea. No matter how he acted, in my opinion, he belonged to no American ethnic group. He appeared Oriental, but knew nothing about the Orient, either. In my mind, Jim was much happier than Wilson despite having suffered discrimination. I speculated that this was probably because Jim had a clearcut identity, whereas Wilson, on the other hand, was a marginal man belonging nowhere.

Almost a decade later, I was to find similar racial discrimination in 1974 in the east central Mississippi town, Hilltown, during my field work with the Choctaw Indians. As I have described already, Indians and blacks were subjected to racial segregation in public places. Some restaurants were barred to nonwhites. The movie theater did not charge the same fees to everyone, thus assuring the segregated seating of Indians and blacks in the balcony. I will never forget the embarrassing scene of the Choctaw student who attempted not to show me the pattern of racial segregation. If the Choctaw youngster had asked me what changes in racial attitudes had occurred during the last decade or so, I would not have had adequate words to explain changes in that particular town. If he had pursued further to ask whether Hilltown, as a part of the South, was the last hope of America, I would not have been prepared to answer. I could have said only that the South was not unifaceted but multifaceted, having good and bad and all that lies between, just as any other region of the nation.

Despite my observations of racial discrimination exhibited toward others, I wish to emphasize that I have never been subjected to it during my ten years of living in the South. It is true, though, that southerners are more openly ambivalent about foreigners. Hence, they often more visibly display their curiosity about foreigners. Sometimes, whites have refused to shake my hand or to have close contact. On a few occasions, I was addressed as "Chinaman." In some rural shopping centers, groups of children have followed me and watched. Now and then, my children have complained that their peers in school addressed them with clichés and epithets. However, these incidents should not be interpreted in terms of racial discrimination. Such curiosities in relation to foreigners are rather natural.

In fact, long before I learned about the phenomenon called racial discrimination, I manifested similar curiosity about Americans. Immediately after World War II, during the American military rule of Korea, I first met an American G.I. in a post office. It was quite a cultural shock to see blue eyes and a projected nose. I had never seen human beings with such odd features. I ran to find my friends and told them about the stranger. My friends and I followed the G.I. wherever he went until he gave us chewing gum to get rid of us. Another time, when I was riding a train soon after the Korean War, I found the train was overcrowded. There was only one vacant seat right beside an American G.I. No one wanted to take the seat next to him. I and others stood up for several hours on that trip, yet we did not act to take the seat. This was not racial segregation by any means. The reason why I did not sit beside him was that I did not feel comfortable around a foreigner. Hence I can fully understand why some southerners have been reluctant to interact with me closely while I was in the field.

Excepting such curiosity and uneasy feelings toward me as a foreigner, I have never been prevented systematically by any southerner from access to the everyday life patterns of the South. Certainly, this does not mean that I was fully accepted by the people in each community as a full participating member. I was always welcome as a foreigner wherever I went. In the field, I was seen as a foreigner, and because of that, was commonly assisted far beyond what I could expect. Southerners showed an eagerness to help me with my field work. Even in a town known to have a tough racial perspective, I was treated very well. But I have been excluded from most traditional customs. Commonly, there was a conditional acceptance relative to my remaining a foreigner and maintaining my foreign identity. On many occasions, I have been asked whether or not I was an American citizen. Whenever I indicated that I was not and had a plan to go back to my home country, the inquirers became very pleased and even more helpful.

Also, I observed differences in the responses of southerners during my previous two field work experiences. When I was studying the pulpwood workers as a graduate student, I received considerable assistance from the native people who knew me as a foreign student helping my professor. In contrast, when I was in charge of twelve students and conducting field work for the Choctaw Indians in Mississippi, the community's eagerness to assist my work was significantly reduced. But when southerners understood me to be a naturalized American citizen, they attempted to treat me as a member of a minority group rather than as a foreigner. This is also true of other foreigners, especially blacks. One of my students who came from Nigeria told me about his experiences during his stay in the South. He had resided in both the North and the South. According to his account, while in the North, it did not matter whether he came from Africa or anywhere else; he was treated as a black. But in the South he had been treated much better after he became identified as a foreign student from Africa.

I still have a strong feeling of being an outsider, although I have been well received as a foreign guest. When my son and I went to the community ball park in the town where I live now, an inquisitive little boy asked my son, "Where 're you from?" I waited interested to see how my son would answer the question. He hesitated, thought, and answered, "I'm from Korea." Literally, he did not come from Korea, for he was born in Atlanta, Georgia, and has never been in Korea. I said to him later, "You didn't come from Korea, you know." He quickly replied, "What else could I have answered, then?" My son intuitively knew what the boy was asking, probably because he had been asked similar questions previously. I figured other first-generation immigrants who speak a foreign language or look different have felt the same feeling—that of being a marginal person in American society.

Since I have tried to conform to the role of the stereotyped Asian both in my field work and in all other aspects of my life, I have yet to become an assimilated member of American society. If being addressed by one's first name is related to the degree of closeness or familiarity, then, this obvious measurement of social distance accurately reflects my position. Although I have taught for five years in the same school, most of the faculty on the campus still address me as "mister" or "doctor" or, less often, "professor." A slight embarrassment arose once after mutual agreement with a colleague that we would address each other on a first-name basis. When next we met, I addressed him thus, but he did not return the greeting similarly. So, I did not do it the next time, which left us back at the original point. Since the manner of addressing a person is an important factor for the functional interrelationship of two people's behavior, my contact is formal so long as I am addressed formally. Thus I have remained a marginal man even in the university community.

Some writers (e.g., Gunnar Myrdal) have indicated that southerners are "informal."[8] This observation differs from mine. Southerners are very formal in many respects, not only in their attitudes toward foreigners, as my experience indicates, but also toward one another. If one wonders about this, he ought to go to a football game at a major southern university. Even if the weather is really warm in early autumn, there is a coat-and-tie audience, excepting the students. Further, in the South both parents and teachers strongly emphasize etiquette, and coach children to say "sir" and "ma'am" properly. Such formality combined with the relatively static and defensive nature of southerners' attitudes govern almost every aspect of the lives of southerners and make it difficult for a foreigner to participate fully in community activities. Traditionally, the southerners have left the least room for immigrants. Hence immigrant communities are not an integral part of the southern scene. Considering that, and with no other visible racial groups other than the blacks and Indians who are both still segregated, the "melting pot" has not become a reality in the South.

My reaction is not only the case for a foreigner but is also the experience of some Yankees. A few years ago, one of my colleagues who was born, raised, and educated in New England related to me that he was experiencing a strong alienation in the local community and its surroundings. He had long hair and maintained very liberal values. Thus, he told me, whenever he went into town stores, native townspeople identified him as a Yankee and treated him differently. He complained that he was the subject of local gossip. Even in the classroom, he had difficulty understanding southern accents. At the same time, a sizable number of his students had difficulty adjusting to his Yankee accent. He was deeply frustrated.

The Yankee told me he would leave the South after only one year because of his frustration. I told him if he stayed longer he would like the South very much. Historically, it might be true that the Yankee has been the chief target of white southern prejudice. But as I told him, that is no longer true in accordance with my observations. Since the beginning of World War II, much of the growth and the increasing prosperity of the South has been accompanied and sustained by the migration of white people from the north as permanent residents. I told him a new southern saying: "In the past the Yankees came down to the South to see the South, but now they are coming down to live for good." He did not intend to take my suggestion. He retorted that I had been treated much better than he, although I was a foreigner. He told me that northerners would never discriminate in such a way against the southerners if they moved to the North. Relative to his remark, I introduced the story of the reception of a southerner at a northern university as a new faculty member, citing the writing of Peter Rose about Lewis Killian:

Lewis Killian once told me that, when he first came to the University of Massachusetts, he moved through a reception line for new faculty. Ahead of him were several Europeans. Despite thick accents, they were greeted without comment. When he got to the head of the line and introduced himself, he was asked if he longed for home. At that point, he reports, he did.[9]

Killian was born, raised, and partly educated in Georgia. If that was the case in a northern university, one could scarcely claim that northerners are much more open-minded to the southerners than vice versa. The Yankee was not happy about my remark and called me an "adopted white southerner." And indeed, after one academic year, he left the department for New England without telling anyone.

The Yankee referred to me as an "adopted white southerner" because he was unable to get my sympathy when he was talking about the South.

Regardless of how he determined my position in the southern community, he would never understand my inner feelings of being an Oriental and a foreigner. In all honesty, as I manifested elsewhere, I have been and am a marginal person in the South instead of an adopted white southerner. I have never deluded myself that I belonged to the native groups of southerners—the whites, blacks, or Indians. In order to conform to the expectation of the natives in the field, I had to behave as a foreigner so that I could get maximum assistance from them for successful field work.

Also, to reduce unnecessary competition with anybody in my school and community, I have again remained a humble foreigner in that setting as well. Even in the classroom with my students, I feel I am an outsider. Once when I was explaining the ethnography of divorce in a crosscultural perspective, I said that "in our society the divorce rate is increasing." Immediately, one student raised his hand and asked me to verify the term "our," whether I referred to Korean society or American society. I had used "our" for American society. But, the student had gotten confused. Since then I have avoided using "our" in the classroom. Having two American-born sons and ten years of residence in the American South was not enough to break down the barrier between "our" and "your." At the same time, I know that I can no longer comfortably fit into my native Korean society. Thus I remain a marginal man who belongs nowhere. Now I understand the truth of Rosalie Wax's writing, and let me repeat it here, that "becoming a member of a society or culture of living people is always a joint process, involving numerous accommodations and adjustments by both the field worker and the people who accept him."[10]

As Myrdal has indicated, "'the southern gentleman,' 'the southern lady,' and 'southern hospitality' are proverbial, even if stereo-typed."[11] Nevertheless, most southerners are courteous, particularly to the foreign guest. Sometimes, southern hospitality to a foreigner can be so generous that the foreigner becomes suspicious and attributes underlying motives that are nonexistent. Some overly sensitive foreigners might interpret the generosity to be a peculiar form of southern prejudice. As a result, some foreigners might wittingly or unwittingly abuse southern hospitality.

I have never failed to recognize the existence of southern hospitality throughout my intensive contacts with southerners in the field or the community where I now live. I confess that I have taken advantage of southern hospitality during my field work. Knowing that southerners would show their hospitality to foreigners, I have behaved in the ways expected of an Oriental. As a result I was able to finish my field work in southern communities without insurmountable difficulties. In fact, if my field work in the South has been successful, it was not owing to excellent training in anthropology or to an exceptional ability to conduct field work under any circumstances, but to the southern hospitality that southerners have proudly inherited from their ancestors for generations.

Just as there are many "Souths," there are many forms of southern hospitality. The motel receptionist voluntarily supplied an enormous amount of information to me during my stay in Pinetown, Georgia. When I finished my field work and was ready to leave the town, I saw tears come to her eyes. I remember uncountable numbers of southerners there who whenever I asked directions kindly took me to the localities personally. A kind dealer dispatched one of his office workers to assist my field work almost on a full-time basis. Although my field work in Pinetown was financed by the funding agency, I was offered free meals on many occasions. When I had an infected ear and visited a local physician, he treated me without any charge for his professional service after his nurse had given me priority over the other patients waiting to see the physician. When I ate meals in a restaurant in Hilltown, Mississippi, the owner of the restaurant would usually sit across the table from me knowing that I was alone and would probably like companionship. If I stopped for a drink when I became thirsty, he would give me a fresh cup of coffee without charge. The motel owner usually gave me a discount rate for my room and an extra desk for my writing. My personal checks were accepted without hesitation. Most of all, I have almost always been received by the southerners with cordiality, warmth, and big smiles.

Certainly, this does not mean that every southerner was hospitable. Some of them expressed uneasy feelings toward me. Some refused to exchange handshakes with me. Quite a few southerners thought of me as being a different kind of man because of my appearance.

When I use the term "southern hospitality," I refer mainly to the warm and friendly reception of white southerners toward my presence in their homes or communities. Although the responses of the white southerners were not uniform during my field work, most of them were cordial. In regard to their attitudes toward other ethnic or racial groups, for instance,

Melvin Tumin analyzed the racial attitudes of the southerners and found them to correlate with education and age.[12] Donald Matthews and James Prothro also observed that education was the most important variable in decreasing racial segregation in the South.[13] However, their studies related to the attitudes of whites toward blacks. There had been no systematic study dealing with the attitudes of whites toward nonblack minority groups. Throughout my field work and residence in the South, I have found that southern hospitality has generally been extended to me relative to the education levels of the people. There are different responses from the highly, marginally, and poorly educated. At the same time, the responses of those three ranges differ by race.

The most highly educated white southerners receive me conditionally. As a result of their wide-ranging experiences, they are the most empathetic of whites in regard to my role as a resident in their community who must conduct his field work in English, although it is difficult. They try to understand my problems and my work, to display sympathy and interest in me, and to assist me when they can. But they are cautious.

This group does not feel threatened by me and cares not what I do in their community so long as I do not attempt to destroy their established norms or aspire to be a full-fledged member of their society with equal station. As the social, political and economic elite in their community, they are in no way ready to relinquish their positions and are to some degree suspect of any newcomer, especially an educated one and certainly a foreign, educated one. Because they are aware that the South is not introduced fairly to outsiders, particularly to foreigners, they are making a conscious effort to change the image of the South and thus treat a foreign guest well. As long as I behave as a foreigner, I have no problems getting along with them, although this group applies the strongest pressure on me to remain a foreigner and not become immersed in American society.

White, blue-collar workers with a marginal education are the most difficult southern whites with whom to work in the field. Having some education, they are not ignorant about the outside world, yet show little interest in foreigners. It sometimes seems they know just enough to be dangerous. That is, they know enough to comprehend sophisticated words and actions but not enough to perceive their context. To them, almost any scholarly activity, whether it be research or investigation, is useless and simply a waste of time. They are invariably the most frustrated group of people in their community. And, doubtlessly, this frustration has been the most important factor in the development of white supremacy attitudes.

Although these people take great pride in their normal native intelligence or common sense, they prefer to avoid members of the university community. They think that any person, idea, or issue must be considered dangerous or at least suspect when there is variance from their frame of reference. Any scholarly argument or national issue is only acceptable to the degree that it conforms to their values and standards. Usually covertly, if not unconsciously, this group of white southerners clings to the belief that the United States is and should be a white man's society. They do not want to see any nonwhite having free access to their community for any purpose. Thus as an Asian I have received a minimum of hospitality from them. Sometimes, they refuse altogether to have contact with me, socially or physically.

The least educated group of white southerners, who also constitute the lower class,[14] receives me the most warmly. Before becoming involved in my field work, I honestly thought this group would be the most difficult with whom to interact. Instead, they are the most gentle southerners. They are the ones who show the most curiosity about me as an Asian anthropologist, and cooperate the most when they can. The hospitality of this group is genuine. Their manner of expression is frank. They are proud to have an Asian guest in their homes when I visit them. As long as my questions are not personal, they willingly supply information. The university is so out of their reach that they do not have feelings of competition or jealousy. They understand research to be both good and necessary. Sometimes, their questions and answers are cautious or whimsical, but never hostile. By and large, their hospitality is absolute and unconditional. Of whites, I am most indebted to the hospitality of this group.

Unfortunately, I have not been able to contact enough highly educated blacks in the field to determine a trend, possibly because few blacks in the South are highly educated. However, it is unlikely that highly educated blacks support the attitudes of highly educated whites because of such things as job discrimination and their exclusion from local government and civic clubs. In most small southern towns, certainly the towns in which I carried on my field work, the blacks do not actively participate socially and politically. When I have manifested my view supporting black participation in local governments, the whites answer by saying that there are few blacks who are qualified to take such posts.

In fact, most small-town blacks who achieve a high status economically and socially through higher education usually leave such towns for urban centers. Many poor and uneducated blacks complain that as soon as those blacks achieve their new statuses, they cut themselves off from their poor and uneducated fellows, one of whom told me, "I'd rather beg to a wealthy white rather than a wealthy black if I've got to." In any event, it is unfortunate that I have been unable to evaluate educated blacks in relation to field experiences.

Throughout my contacts with blacks outside the field setting, those who are highly educated have been much less friendly than their white counterparts. They offer me no sympathy as a member of a minority group undergoing hardships, saying, "We broke through more difficult situations than you have gone through; we broke an iron barrier." On many occasions, I am told that unlike them, I am not entitled to equal treatment because I am not an American citizen. Statements are often made by educated blacks that foreigners are treated much better than native blacks.[15] Also, they suggest that foreigners take their jobs, so that job opportunities for blacks are reduced. Generally, there is a total lack of curiosity relative to foreigners, and southern hospitality does not exist. Whenever I communicate with them, I become even more cautious than with educated whites unless I am disparaging whites.

Blacks having a marginal education show considerable interest in my work in the field. But they remain aloof in personal relations. Obviously, they are the equivalent of highly educated whites in their manner of receiving a foreigner. This group has learned how to survive in the white-dominated society. They are more skillful in their treatment of other racial groups in the midst of the white leadership structure. They know that I have a neutral racial perspective. They are able to realize when I am in the field that I do not represent white values. Occasionally, I am invited into their homes for meals. However, they manipulate the conversation skillfully so they do not expose themselves thoroughly.

The least educated blacks are more difficult for me to deal with in the field. They are more ethnocentric. Indeed, they are strongly held by Americanisms. They know, regardless of their statuses in society, that

America is the only civilized society and the rest of the world is primitive. On occasions, I have been asked by some of this group of blacks whether I had seen a telephone prior to coming to America. Others have asked me whether there are pine trees in Korea, and what their color is. Their mode of expression and manners are alien to me. I really do not know how I should behave around them. An explanation of my field work is useless. It does not make sense to them. Often, I cannot understand their manner of speech, and they have a terrible problem understanding my English with its thick, foreign accent. Frequently, the conversation between this group of blacks and myself reaches a deadlock because of the block in communication.

In 1967–68, when I was working for an OEO evaluation project in metropolitan Atlanta as a research staff member of the Center for Research in Social Change at Emory University, I confessed to the director that I had difficulty understanding the conversation of the poorly educated blacks. The director eased my feeling by saying, "Don't worry about it. No one in our research center understands it any better than you do. What you need is a little bit of imagination and guess what they would say when they speak." The problem I had was not just with their pronunciation of English but also in their manner of speaking.

I have realized throughout my enculturation into middle-class American manners that Americans, especially southerners, tend to be very diplomatic when they speak. They avoid any straightforward expressions if possible. Even in refusal, Americans will say, "No, thank you." The English language itself is very diplomatic. Nevertheless, this group of blacks prefers to use the most simple, direct, and straightforward manner of expression. Sometimes, it is easy to draw the correct conclusion. But, sometimes, one might find oneself suddenly in a puzzling situation.

Hence among this group the virtue of humbleness does not work out very well. If I am humble in my manner, they are likely to look down on me. Surprisingly, this group of blacks encourages directly or indirectly the build-up of white supremacy in the South. They are exceptionally gentle and humble to the point of being servile to the whites. But they are condescending toward other racial groups. My difficulty in dealing with them lies in their lack of opinions and attitudes toward specific issues. I have learned throughout my extensive contact with this group of blacks that I must dress up with a coat and tie when I contact them. Then, they tend to treat me much better. Even so, I learn very little from them, for they readily agree with me without giving any opinions of their own. They seem to not want to bother to think.

The Choctaw Indians of Tennessee and Mississippi have shown me the warmest welcome of the three racial groups in the South. Because of our physical similarity they feel a closeness to me. Reciprocally, I feel a lot easier when I contact them. Often, they seem to be the researchers rather than the respondents. They are interested in me and my native culture. They really show curiosity about the Orient. Although it is located far away from this New World, they wonder how they can look morphologically more like the Orientals than any other racial group. Not many Choctaws are aware of the theory that American Indians migrated from Asia. However, they have vague notions that the Asians and American Indians resemble each other.

Many of the most highly educated Choctaw Indians are not particularly friendly or receptive to my presence on the reservation. They identify me as an anthropologist, instead of an Asian visitor. This group of Choctaws challenged the research project I was conducting, considering it a violation of the civil rights of the Indians. Some refused to be the respondents of anthropologists. They maintain strong beliefs that their conventional leadership has compromised too much with the white leadership structure. They believe themselves to be the emerging group of new leaders. The whites living on the fringe of the reservation consider this group of Indians to be radicals. In the earlier stage of my field work on the reservation, I got negligible assistance from this group of Choctaw Indians. For instance, the college students who were assigned to assist my field work as interpreters and guides were very uncooperative until they understood the whole purpose of the project.

I have been received best by the marginally educated Choctaws. This group is not as sophisticated as the highly educated group. But they are not ignorant of the outside world. They hold to their traditional ways while trying to adjust their lives to the changing world. Since they are so aware of their traditional culture, they are more interested than the others in me and about my native culture. As I recall my native customs and culture, they show a real eagerness to know about it. They are cordial and congenial to me as a person, and they were very cooperative during my field work. I owe a great deal to this group for keeping me relatively comfortable during my stay at the reservation.

The least educated Choctaws tend to be ambivalent at best toward outsiders, including myself. Most of this group occupy low levels in the community structure socially, politically, and economically. For them, proximity of physical features is not a matter of convergence. And from this group of the Choctaws, I do not expect hospitality. They do not believe any form of research or type of policy for the Indians helps them. Since they are not happy, I can not expect a warm welcome from them. They are often hostile toward local whites, outsiders, even fellow Choctaws, including members of their families. To them, southern hospitality is as foreign as I am, and everybody appears to be a stranger.

As I have just depicted, there are many different southerners. In addition, there are black mayors, white liberals, non-Choctaw Indians, Jews, Mexicans, transplanted Yankees, and marginal Orientals. Indeed, the southerners are a heterogeneous lot. Hence any attempt to summarize the South and southerners in a few pages would be an act of temerity. If any one believes there is a homogeneous, one-sided South, his belief is operating within a fallacious frame of reference. The stolid, homogeneous, and unique features attributed to the South no longer exist, if, indeed, they ever did.

As a result of my field work and extensive contacts with numerous southerners, I have obviously concluded that the South is multifaceted. However, beyond that, the South is neither a backward region of the nation nor the region that is the last hope for Americans. Certainly, it is no longer an exotic or virgin American land. The southerners use the same vending machines as Americans outside the South. Every evening the major national television networks carry the news of the day into the living rooms of the southerners, including the news reported about the South on occasion. Even if the news about the South is inaccurate, they will stay tuned and hear the media's version of the southern story instead of turning it off.

There has been a strong move across the nation to force the South to change. Whether in response to this pressure or simply because of national trends, the South has changed, is changing, and will change in the future. When I first came to Atlanta, Georgia, in 1965, there was no basis for believing the city could have a black mayor within ten years. Changes have come faster than anyone could have predicted. As a matter of fact, the rate of change is so rapid that I am reluctant to delineate my portrait of the South at this point in time. For I realize as I finish this book that my description of the several southern communities in which I carried on my field work will soon no longer be adequate.

Nevertheless, Max Weber has observed:

In science, each of us knows that what he has accomplished will be antiquated in ten, twenty, fifty years. That is the fate to which science is subjected; it is the very meaning of scientific work, to which it is devoted in a quite specific sense, as compared with other spheres of culture for which in general the same holds. Every scientific "fulfilment" raises new "questions"; it asks to be "surpassed" and outdated. Whoever wishes to serve science has to resign himself to this fact. Scientific works certainly can last as "gratifications" because of their artistic quality, or they may remain important as a means of training. Yet they will be surpassed scientifically—let that be repeated—for it is our common fate and, more, our common goal.[16]

It is my hope that this work has in some way contributed to that common purpose.

Notes

Notes for the Prologue:
Resocialization but Nonimmersion

1. Upon completion of the project, I shared my experiences with fellow Koreans via radio broadcast. At the request of a publisher, I wrote about my field experiences. Incidently, the publisher later became my father-in-law.

2. According to the survey made by Wilfrid C. Bailey, "At the present time it is possible to earn a degree in anthropology at only 49 schools in the South. Seven offer a minor and 23 have a concentration in anthropology through another degree program, usually sociology. The BA is available at 26 schools, the MA is the highest degree at 11, and 12 award the Ph.D. Three additional schools permit a concentration in anthropology within a sociology Ph.D. program." See Wilfrid C. Bailey, "Anthropology in Southern Colleges and Universities," *The Southern Anthropologist* 1 (1971), 4. During the six years since Bailey made his study, these figures have changed; for example, the University of Tennessee now offers a Ph.D. in anthropology. Even so, higher degrees in anthropology are still limited in southern schools.

3. Historically, the southern cities that had been insignificant before 1861, like Birmingham and Atlanta, are becoming great industrial and commercial cities. See Lewis M. Killian, *White Southerners,* 29.

4. See Virginius Dabney, *Below the Potomac,* 315. See also Ralph McGill, *The South and the Southerner,* 208.

5. H. L. Mencken, *A Mencken Chrestomathy,* 184.

6. *Ibid.,* 185, 186.

7. Lewis Killian shares a similar view on higher education in the South that "southern universities have tried to improve their national images by recruiting faculty and graduate students from outside the region, implicitly admitting to a conception that brands higher education in the South as provincial and inferior." See Killian, *White Southerners,* 84.

8. See Ernest W. Burgess, "Residential Segregation in American Cities," *The Annals of the American Academy of Political and Social Science* 140 (1928), 110.

9. Gunnar Myrdal, *An American Dilemma,* 615.

10. Killian, *White Southerners*, 16.

11. Lewis Killian says that "the great division in the South was between black and white." *Ibid.*, 16.

12. Mencken, *A Mencken Chrestomathy*, 186.

13. Russell W. Middleton, "Racial Problems and the Recruitment of Academic Staff at Southern Colleges and Universities," *American Sociological Review* 26 (1961), 960–70.

14. *Ibid.*, 965.

15. *Ibid.*

16. See Edgar G. Murphy, *Problems of the Present South*, 23.

17. See Rosalie H. Wax, *Doing Fieldwork*, 14.

18. *Ibid.*

19. R.H. Lowie, *The History of Ethnological Theory*, 232. See also Cora DuBois, "Studies in an Indian Town," in *Women in the Field*, ed. Peggy Golde, 219–36.

20. E.E. Evans-Pritchard, *Social Anthropology and Other Essays*, 77–79.

21. Wax, *Doing Fieldwork*, 43.

22. A similar experience of this sort has been noted by Hortense Powdermaker about her field work in Hollywood. Her access to respondents was arranged through formal appointments. See Hortense Powdermaker, *Stranger and Friend*, 209–31.

23. William Whyte has noted similar experiences in his work on *Street Corner Society*. When he used a string of obscenities and profanity in his conversation with his friend, people looked at him with an expression of surprise and disappointment, suggesting that he should not do that. They expected Whyte to be different, and to keep his identity. See William F. Whyte, *Street Corner Society*, 304.

24. I do not use "native" as a derogatory term. It does not connote intellectual, cultural, social, economical, political, or personal inferiority or superiority toward any group to which it is applied. It merely describes people living in an area or country.

25. Lewis Killian indicates that "there is no easy answer for it is ever difficult to define 'the South' as a region (See Killian, *White Southerners*, 10)." However, Howard Odum limits the area to the Old South, which included the states of Va., N.C., S.C., Ky., Tenn., Ga., Fla., Ala., Miss., La., and Ark. See Howard W. Odum, *Southern Regions of the United States*, 219.

26. "In fact, we find very few anthropologists who have published their personalized experiences in the field." See Carole E. Hill, "Graduate Education in Anthropology," *Human Organization* 33 (1974), 409.

27. Social research involving direct observation in the researcher's own society was carried on in England and France as early as the latter part of the eighteenth century. However, the most obvious trend emerging in American society has been documented by American anthropologists in the form of contemporary community studies, i.e., Lynds' *Middletown;* Warner's and his associates' *Yankee City* series and *Jonesville;* Davis' and Gardner's *Deep South;* Dollard's *Caste and Class in a Southern Town;* and West's *Plainville U.S.A.*, have been influential in the switch from the primitive scene to the contemporary American communities.

28. Killian, *White Southerners*, xi.

29. Cornelius Osgood, *The Koreans and Their Culture*, passim.

30. Vincent S.R. Brandt, *A Korean Village,* passim.
31. Powdermaker, *Stranger and Friend,* 13.
32. Alexis de Tocqueville, *Democracy in America,* passim.
33. James Bryce, *The American Commonwealth,* passim.
34. Myrdal, *An American Dilemma,* passim.

Notes for Chapter 1
Field Work among Pulpwood Workers

1. Frequently, the research topic of a graduate student is related to the interest of his major professor. Thomas Williams indicates that "the factors that determine which society to study vary between anthropologists. The choice of an anthropologist completing his doctoral degree to live and study in a geographic region and with a particular people often depends upon the research interests and expectations of the professors who guide his graduate training." See Thomas Rhys Williams, *Field Methods in the Study of Culture,* 4.

2. See Wilfrid C. Bailey, "Science and Humanism: Involvement in Contemporary Affairs," in *Crisis on Campus,* eds. Russell B. Nye *et al.,* 129–55.

3. George Foster reveals that "applied anthropology enjoys less prestige than does theoretically oriented anthropology." See George M. Foster, *Applied Anthropology,* ix.

4. In May 1964 the Society for Applied Anthropology set up a committee on ethics to draw up a specific code by which professional applied anthropologists could work. The code specifies the responsibilities of the applied anthropologist toward various people involved in his work. See L. R. Peattie, "Interventionism and Applied Science in Anthropology," *Human Organization* 17(1958), 4–8.

5. Hill, "Graduate Education in Anthropology," 409.

6. See Powdermaker, *Stranger and Friend,* 10. Also see Irwin T. Sanders, "Research with Peasants in Underdeveloped Areas," *Social Forces* 35(1956), 1.

7. It would be useful to conduct preliminary observations for the intensive study. See Williams, *Field Methods,* 20.

8. See John Beattie, *Understanding an African Kingdom;* Gerald D. Berreman, *Behind Many Masks;* Elenore Bowen, *Return to Laughter;* R. Henry and S. Saberwal, eds. *Stress and Response in Fieldwork;* B. Malinowski, *A Diary in the Strict Sense of the Term;* D. Maybury-Lewis, *The Savage and the Innocent;* Powdermaker, *Stranger and Friend;* Williams, *Field Methods;* M. Freilich, *Marginal Natives;* Peggy Golde, ed. *Women in the Field;* Wax, *Doing Fieldwork.*

9. A cord is a unit of measurement of stacked wood. A standard pulpwood cord contains 128 cubic feet. However, woodyards purchase wood by weight according to a formula based on the type of wood.

10. See Pertti J. Pelto, *Anthropological Research,* 227.

11. *Ibid.,* 229.

12. A producer as a local term is an individual who operates or manages pulpwood harvesting crews, owns pulpwood harvesting equipment, and sells pulpwood either directly

to a mill or to a dealer who is an intermediate agent buying wood from producers and reselling it to a mill.

13. Pelto, *Anthropological Research*, 142–46. See also Williams, *Field Methods*, 7–8.

14. See Powdermaker, *Stranger and Friend*, 157–58.

15. *Ibid.*, 52.

16. The use of key informants as sources of information about the culture and people being studied has been a mainstay in most anthropological field work. "A fieldworker's most important informants are frequently persons who occupy specialized positions in the local society." See Pelto, *Anthropological Research*, 98. Also see Williams, *Field Methods*, 29.

17. Gunnar Myrdal has stated that in the 1940s "the lumber industry is really nothing but an out-growth of agriculture." See Myrdal, *An American Dilemma*, 1092.

18. The term, "longwood," is a local term. It is often referred to as a "tree-length," meaning an entire tree with the exception of the unmerchantable top and limbs, suitable for lumber, pulpwood, or other wood products. See W. S. Bromley, *Pulpwood Production*, 225.

19. According to the agriculture extension agents of the county, in 1969, 100,000 cords of wood were harvested. About 80 percent, or 331 square miles, of the county is covered with commercial forests.

20. Often approval of well-known and respected local leaders has led to successful anthropological field work. See Powdermaker, *Stranger and Friend*, 140–43; Williams, *Field Methods*, 14; Julia G. Crane and Michael V. Angrosino, *Field Projects in Anthropology*, 15.

21. "In many studies, the community used as a field, has been chosen as much for its convenience as for its representativeness." See Conrad M. Arensberg and Solon T. Kimball, *Culture and Community*, 9.

22. Margaret Mead speculates that a lack of suspicion while she was working in New Guinea may have suggested that the people felt no threat by a woman anthropologist. See Margaret Mead, "Field Work in the Pacific Islands, 1925–1967," in *Women in the Field*, ed. Peggy Golde, 293–331.

23. Howard W. Odum, *The Way of the South*, 6–7.

24. Geologically, Pinetown is a part of the Atlantic Coastal Plain, underlaid by stratified sedimentation. This sedimentation consists of alternating beds of unconsolidated and semi-consolidated clay, silt, sand, limestone, and dolomite. The climate of Pinetown is typical of South Georgia. The rainfall averages about 47 inches per year. The annual average temperature is between 67 and 68 degrees F. About 260 days are frost-free. Owing to the geological and climatic conditions, the longleaf and slash pines are well-suited to this area and have become the major forest resources of the region.

25. Conrad M. Arensberg, "American Communities," *American Anthropologist* 57 (1955), 1151.

Notes for Chapter II
Living in Pinetown, Georgia

1. See Powdermaker, *Stranger and Friend*, 56.

2. Killian, *White Southerners*, 65.

3. Burgess, "Residential Segregation in American Cities," 110. See also Myrdal, *An American Dilemma*, 620.

4. Dollard, *Caste and Class*, 180.

5. Myrdal, *An American Dilemma*, 615.

6. Pertti Pelto, while describing the sexual problems of anthropologists during their field work, said, "Sexual relations are an important aspect of amicable ties within communities, and it is not uncommon for the anthropologist to be offered access to females as a gesture of friendship. Such a situation presents the fieldworker with a complex dilemma: sexual involvement with local women can lead to serious difficulties; on the other hand, to refuse can be interpreted as an unfriendly act." See Pelto, *Anthropological Research*, 226. And see also Beattie, *Understanding an African Kingdom*, 16; Colin Turnbull, *The Forest People*, 143.

7. Common practice among anthropologists nowadays is to code names of informants and use the code instead of a name in field notes so that if the notes are lost, confidential information is not revealed. Frankly, I was not aware of this practice.

8. In the South, even in greeting and responses, the polite additive "sir" or "ma'am" usually accompanies the addressee's name. This appears to be used principally by those of elevated social status. See James Spears, "Southern Folk Greetings and Responses," *Mississippi Folklore Register* 8 (1974), 219.

9. "Variation in racial segregation and discrimination has been a result not only of different local traditions but also the number and proportion of the minority group in terms of the presence and absence dichotomy." See Myrdal, *An American Dilemma*, 615.

10. The Negro-as-an-American is exposed to norms of prejudice and discrimination toward minority groups. In fact, there is some indication that minority groups may be more prejudiced toward one another than is the case of the dominant groups toward any particular minority. Louis Lomax, for instance, describes the attitude of blacks toward Jews. See Louis E. Lomax, *The Negro Revolt*, 179–80.

11. "In the spring following the Japanese attack on the U.S. fleet at Pearl Harbor, all of the Japanese Americans residing on the Pacific Coast were incarcerated by order of the U.S. government. . . . After keeping them jammed in assembly centers in California, the authorities decided to ship them to relocation centers in isolated sections of the West and Midwest until circumstances should permit their release or some other expedient should present itself." See Wax, *Doing Fieldwork*, 59. And see also Morton Grodzins, *Americans Betrayed;* Dorothy Swain Thomas and Richard S. Nishimoto, *The Spoilage*.

12. The average family size of blacks in the rural South is 4.33, and 20 percent of the families contain more than 7 persons in accordance with the U.S. Census of 1970.

13. For further descriptions of the characteristics of black houses in the southern rural communities, see Sally Belfrage, *Freedom Summer*, 39; Alphonso Pinkney, *Black Americans*, 56–60; Elizabeth Sutherland, ed. *Letters from Mississippi*, 39–41.

14. Odum, *Southern Regions of the United States*, 210.

15. See Ernest J. Hopkins, *Mississippi's BAWI Plan*, passim; see also Charles P. Roland, *The Improbable Era*, 11–29.

16. McGill, *The South and the Southerner*, 194.

17. John C. Ransom et al., *I'll Take My Stand*, passim.

18. Louis D. Rubin, Jr., "Regionalism and the Southern Literary Renascence," in *The South and the Sectional Image*, ed. Dewey W. Grantham, 154.

19. Killian, *White Southerners*, 30.

20. William B. Hesseltine and David L. Smiley, *The South in American History*, 399–411.

21. Killian, *White Southerners*, 83–90.

22. *Ibid.*, 84–85.

23. *Ibid.*, 86.

24. "Representatives of industry in the South, even those in the North and speaking for large national corporations, may go so far as to adopt the Federally sponsored 'equal opportunity' policy and genuinely try to make it work, but they made it plain that 'we are not crusaders' (See Munro S. Edmonson and David R. Norsworthy, "Industry and Race in the Southern United States," in *Industrialisation and Race Relations*, ed. Guy Hunter, 52)." Indeed, industrialization in the South does not necessarily lead to greater racial democracy. Perhaps it will, but it has not done so yet. See Herbert Blumer, "Industrialisation and Race Relations," in *Industrialisation and Race Relations*, ed. Guy Hunter, 232.

25. More than 30 years ago, Myrdal indicated that the skilled pulpwood workers, such as sawyers, during the twenties and early thirties, earned more than three or four times per hour, on average, than did the general laborers. According to my observation, Myrdal's information is no longer valid. See Myrdal, *An American Dilemma*, 1092.

Notes for Chapter III
Field Work among Choctaw Indians

1. See Gordon Willey, *An Introduction to American Archaeology*, 12–13; Clark Wissler, *Indians of the United States*, 3–15. And see also the original theory in Samuel Haven, *Archaeology of the United States*.

2. See John H. Peterson, Jr., "The Indian in the Old South," in *Red, White, and Black*, ed. Charles M. Hudson, 116–33.

3. Eileen Maynard, "The Growing Negative Image of the Anthropologist Among American Indians," *Human Organization* 33 (1974), 402–404.

4. Vine Deloria, Jr., *Custer Died for Your Sins*, 84.

5. Roger M. Keesing and Felix M. Keesing, *New Perspectives in Cultural Anthropology*, 369–370.

6. *Ibid.*, 370.

7. Li An-che, "Zuni: Some Observations and Queries," *American Anthropologist* 39 (1937), 62–76.

8. *Ibid.*, 68.

9. John H. Peterson, Jr., "The Mississippi Band of Choctaw Indians" (Ph.D. diss., Univ. of Ga., 1970); Carol E. Austin, "Relationship Between Income and Possession of Consumer Items among Whites, Negroes, and Indians" (M.A. thesis, Univ. of Ga., 1966); Betty C. Ridley, "Relationship Between Family Characteristics and Level of Living of Three Ethnic Groups with Special Emphasis on the Choctaw Indians" (M.A. thesis, Univ. of Ga.,

1965); Lamar E. Ross, "Ethnicity and Cultural Diversity Among Indians, Negroes, and Whites in Mississippi" (M.A. thesis, Univ. of Ga., 1970).

   10. Toptown has a population of 4,794 in accordance with the U.S. Census, 1970. It has been a local marketing center since the early 1900s. Although since 1960 several manufacturing industries, such as electronic appliance factories, have moved in, traditional southern soft industries, i.e., food, apparel, furniture, etc., are the major industries. For the Choctaw Indians, Toptown is the closest marketing center.

   11. According to the 1970 U.S. Census, 33.9 percent of the total population of Riverville County is black, compared with 65.9 percent white and .498 percent Indian. As far as the ratio of the black population in the county is concerned, it is the fourth highest in the state of Tennessee. The proportion of blacks is more than double that of the state (15.8 percent black; 83.9 percent white), and more than triple the figure of the entire nation (11.1 percent black).

   12. Monte Kenaston studied this group of Choctaws in 1967. He calls this village "Bottomville (a pseudonym)" in his dissertation. I did not know the existence of such a study because his dissertation was not completed until 1972. I was much indebted to his work. See Monte Ray Kenaston, "Sharecropping, Solidarity, and Social Cleavage" (Ph.D. diss., Southern Ill. Univ., 1972).

   13. See Joan Ablon, "Relocated American Indians in the San Francisco Bay Area," *Human Organization* 23 (1964), 296–304; Theodore D. Graves and M. Van Arsdale, "Values, Expectations, and Relocation," *Human Organization* 25(1965), 300-307; Theodore D. Graves, "Drinking and Drunkenness Among Urban Indians," in *The American Indian in Urban Society*, eds. J. O. Waddell and Michael Watson, 274–311; Merwyn S. Garbarino, "Life in the City," in *The American Indian in Urban Society*, eds. J. O. Waddell and Michael Watson, 168–205; Joseph G. Jorgensen, "Indians and the Metropolis," in *The American Indian in Urban Society*, eds. J.O. Waddell and Michael Watson, 245–73.

   14. U.S. Congress, *Toward Economic Development for Native American Communities.* Prepared for the Joint Economic Committee by Helen W. Johnson, "American Indians in Rural Poverty" (Washington, D.C.: Government Printing Office, 1969), 35.

   15. The newspaper clipping has used real names, both personal names and the name of the town. In order to keep anonymity, I intentionally deleted them. I am indebted to the description made by Thomas Bevier.

   16. Maynard, "The Growing Negative Image of the Anthropologist Among American Indians," 402.

   17. See Kenaston, "Sharecropping, Solidarity, and Social Cleavage," 21–27.

   18. Peterson, "The Mississippi Band of Choctaw Indians," 191.

   19. John H. Peterson, Jr., "Assimilation, Separation, and Out-migration in an American Indian Group," *American Anthropologist* 74(1972), 1286–95.

   20. Around 1951–52 most of the black sharecroppers in the Riverville area were on strike (personal communication from Robert B. Fegerson, Southern Indian Antiquities Survey, Inc., July 18, 1973).

   21. See migration model of Germani and Hodge. Gino Germani, "Migration and Acculturation," in *Handbook for Social Science Research in Urban Areas*, ed. Phillip M. Hauser,

159–78; William H. Hodge, "Navajo Urban Migration," in *The American Indian in Urban Society*, eds. J.O. Waddell and Michael Watson, 342–91.

22. Kenaston, "Sharecropping, Solidarity, and Social Cleavage," 23.

23. During the two-year period of my contacts, the population of the Riverville Choctaw Indians changed very little.

24. Toptown whites prefer to call the Choctaws tenant farmers, but they are true sharecroppers as Kenaston has described *(Ibid.)*. George Foster, however, calls such a relationship a "patron-client" relationship. See George M. Foster, "The Dyadic Contract in Tzintzuntzan," *American Anthropologist* 65 (1963), 1280–94.

25. Kenaston, "Sharecropping, Solidarity, and Social Cleavage," 66.

26. See Austin, "Relationship Between Income and Possession of Consumer Items Among Whites, Negroes, and Indians"; John H. Peterson, Jr., *Socio-economic Characteristics of the Mississippi Choctaw Indians*, 22.

27. I am indebted to the health representative who assisted me in the completion of the 1974 study on the Choctaws in Riverville.

28. It is the same case among the Choctaws on the reservation in Mississippi. See Peterson, "The Mississippi Band of Choctaw Indians," 151–58.

29. See further details on the matrilineal system of Choctaw Indians in J. R. Swanton, *Source Material for the Social and Ceremonial Life of the Choctaw Indians*, 77–90; Fred Eggan, "Historical Changes in the Choctaw Kinship System," *American Anthropologist* 39(1937), 34–52; Alexander Spoehr, *Changing Kinship Systems*, 151–235; Pamelia A. Coe, "Lost in the Hills of Home" (M.A. thesis, Columbia Univ., 1960).

30. Considering language usage in their homes, almost one-half of the entire Choctaw population in Riverville and its vicinity speak either English predominantly or both languages equally, while 80 percent of the Choctaws on the reservation in Mississippi speak Choctaw predominantly according to the results of my 1974 survey.

31. The original Choctaw kinship system was Crow type, the essential characteristic of which is the classification of a father's sister's female descendants through the females, and the father's sisters' sons with the fathers, thus giving a definite descendant pattern. See the details of Crow type in George P. Murdock, *Social Structure*, 100–241. See also Leslie Spier, *The Distribution of Kinship Systems in North America*, 73–74.

32. Bobby Thompson and John H. Peterson, Jr., "Mississippi Choctaw Identity," in *The New Ethnicity*, ed. John W. Bennett, 179–80.

33. While unilateral descent is the tracing of relationship through either the male or the female, bilateral descent links a person with a group of close relatives through both sexes; it limits the number of close relatives by excluding some of both the father's kinship group and the mother's kinship group. See Ernest L. Schusky, *Manual for Kinship Analysis*, 73, 79.

34. Kenaston, "Sharecropping, Solidarity, and Social Cleavage," 94–100.

35. Lloyd A. Fallers, "Are African Cultivators to Be Called 'Peasants'?" *Current Anthropology* 2(1961), 108–10.

36. George M. Foster, "What is a Peasant?" in *Peasant Society*, eds. Jack M. Potter et al., 2–14.

37. R. Firth, *Elements of Social Organization*, 87.

38. Robert Redfield, *Peasant Society and Culture*, passim; Foster, "What is Folk

Culture?" *American Anthropologist* 55(1953) 159–73; McKim Marriott, "Little Communities in an Indigenous Civilization," in *Village India,* ed. McKim Marriott, 171–222.

39. Fallers, "Are African Cultivators to Be Called 'Peasants'?" 109.

40. See Arthur F. Raper, *Preface to Peasantry,* passim.

41. *Ibid.,* 4.

42. Margaret Park Redfield, ed. *Human Nature and the Study of Society,* 283.

43. Foster, "What is a Peasant?" 6.

44. Margaret Park Redfield, *Human Nature and the Study of Society,* 7.

45. Choong Soon Kim, "Life Patterns of the Off-reservation Choctaws in a West Tennessee Community," (paper delivered at the 9th Annual Meeting of the Southern Anthropological Society, Blacksburg, Va., Apr. 4–6, 1974).

46. Raper, *Preface to Peasantry,* passim.

47. Francis L. K. Hsu, "Prejudice and Its Intellectual Effect in American Anthropology," *American Anthropologist* 75(1973), 5.

48. Francis Hsu has examined several areas of anthropological literature in order to find the scholarly citations for the works of nonwestern anthropologists. His finding indicates that the works referred to were primarily ethnographies by natives of their own cultures. See further details of his analysis in Hsu, "Prejudice and Its Intellectual Effect in American Anthropology," 1–19.

49. *Ibid.,* 5.

50. *Ibid.,* 5–6.

51. *Ibid.,* 1.

Notes for Chapter IV
Going to Hilltown, Mississippi

1. James W. Loewen, *The Mississippi Chinese,* 1.

2. *Ibid.,* 1–2.

3. Nanih Waiya, the Mother Mound, is located near Noxapater, Mississippi. It occupies a unique place in Choctaw tradition, for according to legend it is connected with both the creation and migration of the tribe. The center of Choctaw lands before the advent of the white man, it was considered by Indians to be the birthplace of their race. Out of the mound ages ago, they believe, came the first Muskhogean, Cherokee, and Chikasaw, who sunned on ramparts of the mound and moved eastward. Emerging from Nanih Waiya last were the Choctaws who sunned themselves until dry to settle around the mound—their "great mother" who told them that if ever they left her side, they would die.

4. Peterson, "The Mississippi Band of Choctaw Indians," 1–2.

5. Pelto, *Anthropological Research,* 229.

6. Laura Nader, *Talea and Juquila,* vi.

7. Deloria, *Custer Died for Your Sins,* passim.

8. Maynard, "The Growing Negative Image of the Anthropologist Among American Indians," 403.

Notes for the Epilogue:
The South and Southern Hospitality

1. See Murphy, *Problems of the Present South,* 23.
2. Killian, *White Southerners,* 25.
3. Murphy, *Problems of the Present South,* 23.
4. Killian, *White Southerners,* xi.
5. Some writers do not agree with this view. See John Shelton Reed, *The Enduring South,* 83–90.
6. Killian, *White Southerners,* xi.
7. *Ibid.,* 137.
8. Myrdal, *An American Dilemma,* 459.
9. Killian, *White Southerners,* x.
10. Wax, *Doing Fieldwork,* 43.
11. Myrdal, *An American Dilemma,* 45.
12. Melvin M. Tumin, *Desegregation,* passim.
13. Donald R. Matthews and James W. Prothro, *Negroes and the New Southern Politics,* 343, 349–50.
14. The definition of *class* used here is common sense usage. Since class in industrialized societies is informally judged on the basis of numerous factors, my choice of limited factors is arbitrary and debatable.
15. Some blacks say that "the oft-told story of German prisoners of war being fed in the dining room of a restaurant while Negro soldiers in United States uniforms were served in the kitchen captured the essence of this inconsistency." See Killian, *White Southerners,* 36.
16. Max Weber, "Science As a Vocation," in *The Relevance of Sociology,* ed. Jack D. Douglas, 45.

Bibliography

Ablon, Joan. "Relocated American Indians in the San Francisco Bay Area," *Human Organization* 23(1964), 296–304.

Arensberg, Conrad M. "American Communities," *American Anthropologist* 57(1955), 1143–60.

———, and Solon T. Kimball. *Culture and Community*. New York: Harcourt, 1965.

Austin, Carol E. "Relationship Between Income and Possession of Consumer Items Among Whites, Negroes, and Indians" (M.A. thesis, University of Georgia, 1966).

Bailey, Wilfrid C. "Anthropology in Southern Colleges and Universities," *The Southern Anthropologist* (Newsletter of the Southern Anthropological Society) 1(1971), 1–5.

———. "Science and Humanism: Involvement in Contemporary Affairs." In *Crisis on Campus,* eds. Russell B. Nye *et al.,* 129–55. Bowling Green, Ohio: Bowling Green Univ. Press, 1971.

Beattie, John. *Understanding an African Kingdom*. New York: Holt, 1965.

Belfrage, Sally. *Freedom Summer*. New York: Viking, 1965.

Berreman, Gerald D. *Behind Many Masks*. Monograph 4. Ithaca: Society for Applied Anthropology, 1962.

Blumer, Herbert. "Industrialisation and Race Relations," in *Industrialisation and Race Relations,* ed. Guy Hunter, 220–53. New York: Oxford Univ. Press, 1965.

Bowen, Elenore. *Return to Laughter*. London: Gollancz, 1954.

Brandt, Vincent S. R. *A Korean Village: Between Farm and Sea*. Cambridge, Mass.: Harvard Univ. Press, 1971.

Bromley, W. S. *Pulpwood Production*. Danville, Va.: The Interstate Printers, 1969.

Bryce, James. *The American Commonwealth.* New York: Macmillan, 1911 (orig. 1893).

Burgess, Ernest W. "Residential Segregation in American Cities," *The Annals of the American Academy of Political and Social Science* 140(1928), 105–15.

Coe, Pamelia A. "Lost in the Hills of Home: Outline of Mississippi Choctaw Social Organization" (M.A. thesis, Columbia Univ., 1960).

Crane, Julia G., and Michael V. Angrosino. *Field Projects in Anthropology.* Morristown, N.J.: General Learning Press, 1974.

Dabney, Virginius. *Below the Potomac.* New York: Appleton, 1942.

Davis, Allison, *et al. Deep South: A Social Anthropological Study of Caste and Class.* Chicago: Univ. of Chicago Press, 1941.

Deloria, Vine, Jr. *Custer Died for Your Sins: An Indian Manifesto.* New York: Macmillan, 1969.

Dollard, John. *Caste and Class in a Southern Town.* New Haven: Yale Univ. Press, 1937.

DuBois, Cora. "Studies in an Indian Town." In *Women in the Field,* ed. Peggy Golde, 219–36. Chicago: Aldine Publishing Company, 1970.

Edmonson, Munro S., and David R. Norsworthy. "Industry and Race in the Southern United States," in *Industrialisation and Race Relations,* ed. Guy Hunter, 46–60. New York: Oxford Univ. Press, 1965.

Eggan, Fred. "Historical Changes in the Choctaw Kinship System," *American Anthropologist* 39(1937), 34–52.

Evans-Pritchard, E. E. *Social Anthropology and Other Essays.* New York: Free Press of Glencoe, 1964 (orig. 1951.)

Fallers, Lloyd A. "Are African Cultivators to Be Called Peasant?" *Current Anthropology* 2(1961), 108–10.

Firth, R. *Elements of Social Organization.* London: Watts and Company, 1951.

Foster, George M. "What is Folk Culture?" *American Anthropologist* 55(1953), 159–73.

———. "The Dyadic Contract in Tzintzuntzan, II: Patron-Client Relationship," *American Anthropologist* 65(1963), 1280–94.

———. "What is a Peasant?" in *Peasant Society: A Reader,* eds. Jack M. Potter, *et al.,* 2–14. Boston: Little, 1967.

———. *Applied Anthropology.* Boston: Little, 1969.

Freilich, M. *Marginal Natives: Anthropologist at Work.* New York: Harper, 1970.

Garbarino, Merwyn S. "Life in the City: Chicago." In *The American Indian in Urban Society,* eds. J. O. Waddell and Michael Watson, 168–205. Boston: Little, 1971.

Germani, Gino. "Migration and Acculturation," In *Handbook for Social Science*

Research in Urban Areas, ed. Phillip M. Hauser, 159–78. Paris: UNESCO, 1964.

Golde, Peggy, ed. *Women in the Field.* Chicago: Aldine Publishing Company, 1970.

Graves, Theodore D. "Drinking and Drunkenness Among Urban Indians." In *The American Indian in Urban Society,* eds. J. O. Waddell and Michael Watson, 274–311. Boston: Little, 1971.

————, and M. Van Arsdale. "Values, Expectations, and Relocation: The Navajo Indian Migrant to Denver," *Human Organization* 25(1965), 300–307.

Grodzins, Morton. *Americans Betrayed: Politics and the Japanese Evacuation.* Chicago: Univ. of Chicago Press, 1949.

Haven, Samuel. *Archaeology of the United States.* Washington, D.C.: Smithsonian Institution, 1856.

Henry, R., and S. Saberwal, eds. *Stress and Response in Fieldwork.* New York: Holt, 1969.

Hesseltine, William B., and David L. Smiley. *The South in American History.* Englewood Cliffs, N.J.: Prentice-Hall, 1960.

Hill, Carole E. "Graduate Education in Anthropology: Conflicting Role Identity in Fieldwork," *Human Organization* 33(1974), 408–12.

Hodge, William H. "Navajo Urban Migration." In *The American Indian in Urban Society,* eds. J. O. Waddell and Michael Watson, 342–91. Boston: Little, 1971.

Hopkins, Ernest J. *Mississippi's BAWI Plan: Balance Agriculture with Industry.* Atlanta: Federal Reserve Bank of Atlanta, 1944.

Hsu, Francis L.K. "Prejudice and Its Intellectual Effect in American Anthropology: An Ethnographic Report," *American Anthropologist* 75(1973), 1–19.

Jorgensen, Joseph G. "Indians and the Metropolis." In *The American Indian in Urban Society,* eds. J. O. Waddell and Michael Watson, 66–113. Boston: Little, 1971.

Keesing, Roger M., and Felix M. Keesing. *New Perspectives in Cultural Anthropology.* New York: Holt, 1971.

Kenaston, Monte Ray. "Sharecropping, Solidarity, and Social Cleavage: The Genesis of a Choctaw Sub-community in Tennessee" (Ph.D. diss., Southern Illinois Univ. 1972).

Killian, Lewis M. *White Southerners.* New York: Random, 1970.

Kim, Choong Soon. "Life Patterns of the Off-reservation Choctaws in a West Tennessee Community." (Paper delivered at the 9th Annual Meeting of the Southern Anthropological Society, Blacksburg, April 5, 1974).

Li, An-che. "Zuni: Some Observations and Queries," *American Anthropologist* 39(1937), 62–76.

Loewen, James W. *The Mississippi Chinese: Between Black and White*. Cambridge, Mass.: Harvard Univ. Press, 1971.

Lomax, Louis E. *The Negro Revolt*. New York: Harper, 1962.

Lowie, R. H. *The History of Ethnological Theory*. New York: Farrar and Rinehart, 1937.

Lynd, Robert S., and H. M. Lynd. *Middletown: A Study in Contemporary American Culture*. New York: Harcourt, 1929.

————. *Middletown in Transition: A Study in Cultural Conflicts*. New York: Harcourt, 1937.

Malinowski, B. *A Diary in the Strict Sense of the Term*. New York: Harcourt, 1967.

Marriott, McKim. "Little Communities in an Indigeneous Civilization." In *Village India*, ed. McKim Marriott, 171–222. American Anthropological Association, memoir 83, 1955.

Matthews, Donald R., and James W. Prothro. *Negroes and the New Southern Politics*. New York: Harcourt, 1966.

Maybury-Lewis, D. *The Savage and the Innocent*. London: Evans, 1965.

Maynard, Eileen. "The Growing Negative Image of the Anthropologist Among American Indians," *Human Organization* 33 (1974), 402–404.

McGill, Ralph. *The South and the Southerner*. Boston: Little, 1964 (orig. 1959).

Mead, Margaret. "Field Work in the Pacific Islands, 1925–1967." In *Women in the Field*, ed. Peggy Golde, 293–331. Chicago: Aldine Publishing Company, 1970.

Mencken, H.L. *A Mencken Chrestomathy*. New York: Knopf, 1967.

Middleton, Russell W. "Racial Problems and the Recruitment of Academic Staff at Southern Colleges and Universities," *American Sociological Review* 26 (1961), 960–70.

Murdock, George P. *Social Structure*. New York: Macmillan, 1949.

Murphy, Edgar G. *Problems of the Present South: A Discussion of Certain of the Educational, Industrial, and Political Issues in the Southern States*. New York: Macmillan, 1904.

Myrdal, Gunnar. *An American Dilemma*. New York: Harper, 1944.

Nader, Laura. *Talea and Juquila*. Berkeley and Los Angeles: Univ. of California Publications in Archaeology and Ethnology, 48, 1964.

Odum, Howard W. *Southern Regions of the United States*. Chapel Hill: Univ. of North Carolina Press, 1936.

————. *The Way of the South*. New York: Macmillan, 1947.

Osgood, Cornelius. *The Koreans and Their Culture*. New York: The Ronald Press, 1951.

Peattie, L. R. "Interventionism and Applied Science in Anthropology," *Human Organization* 17(1958), 4–8.

Pelto, Pertti J. *Anthropological Research: The Structure of Inquiry*. New York: Harper, 1970.

Peterson, John H., Jr. "The Mississippi Band of Choctaw Indians: The Recent History and Current Social Relations" (Ph.D. diss., Univ. of Georgia, 1970).

———. *Socio-economic Characteristics of the Mississippi Choctaw Indians*. Social Science Research Center Report No. 34. State College: Mississippi State University, 1970.

———. "The Indian in the Old South." In *Red, White, and Black*, ed. Charles M. Hudson, 116–33. Southern Anthropological Society Proceedings, No. 5. Athens: Univ. of Georgia Press, 1971.

———. "Assimilation, Separation, and Out-migration in an American Indian Group," *American Anthropologist* 74(1972), 1286–95.

Pinkney, Alphonso. *Black Americans*. Englewood Cliffs, N.J.: Prentice-Hall, 1969.

Powdermaker, Hortense. *Stranger and Friend: The Way of an Anthropologist*. New York: Norton, 1966.

Ransom, John C. *et al. I'll Take My Stand*. New York: Harper, 1930.

Raper, Arthur F. *Preface to Peasantry: A Tale of Two Black Belt Counties*. Chapel Hill: Univ. of North Carolina Press, 1936.

Redfield, Margaret Park, ed. *Human Nature and the Study of Society: The Papers of Robert Redfield*, Vol. I. Chicago: Univ. of Chicago Press, 1962.

Redfield, Robert. *The Primitive World and Its Transformations*. Ithaca: Cornell Univ. Press, 1953.

———. *Peasant Society and Culture*. Chicago: Univ. of Chicago Press, 1956.

Reed, John Shelton. *The Enduring South: Subcultural Persistence in Mass Society*. Lexington, Mass.: Lexington Books, 1972.

Ridley, Betty C. "Relationship Between Family Characteristics and Level of Living of Three Ethnic Groups, with Special Emphasis on the Choctaw Indians." (M.A. thesis, Univ. of Georgia, 1965.)

Roland, Charles P. *The Improbable Era: The South since World War II*. Lexington, Ky.: Univ. Press of Kentucky, 1975.

Ross, Lamar E. "Ethnicity and Cultural Diversity Among Indians, Negroes, and Whites in Mississippi." (M.A. thesis, Univ. of Georgia, 1970.)

Rubin, Louis D., Jr. "Regionalism and the Southern Literary Renascence." In *The South and the Sectional Image*, ed. Dewey W. Grantham, 145–60. New York: Harper, 1967.

Sanders, Irwin T. "Research with Peasants in Underdeveloped Areas," *Social Forces* 35(1956), 1–10.

Schusky, Ernest L. *Manual for Kinship Analysis*. New York: Holt, 1965.

Spears, James. "Southern Folk Greetings and Responses," *Mississippi Folklore Register* 8(1974), 218–20.

Spier, Leslie. *The Distribution of Kinship Systems in North America.* Seattle: Univ. of Washington Publications in Anthropology, Vol. 2, No. 2, 1925.

Spoehr, Alexander. *Changing Kinship System: A Study in the Acculturation of the Creeks, Cherokee, and Choctaw.* Chicago: Field Museum of Natural History, Anthropological Series, Vol. 33, No. 4, Publication 583, 1947.

Sutherland, Elizabeth, ed. *Letters from Mississippi.* New York: McGraw-Hill, 1965.

Swanton, J. R. *Source Material for the Social and Ceremonial Life of the Choctaw Indians.* Washington, D.C.: Bureau of American Ethnology Bulletin 103, 1931.

Thomas, Dorothy Swain, and Richard S. Nishimoto. *The Spoilage: Japanese-American Evacuation and Resettlement.* Berkeley: Univ. of California Press, 1946.

Thompson, Bobby, and John H. Peterson, Jr. "Mississippi Choctaw Identity: Genesis and Change." *The New Ethnicity,* ed. John W. Bennett, 179–96. Minneapolis: Westing Publishing Co., 1975 (Annual Proceedings of the American Ethnological Society).

Tocqueville, Alexis de. *Democracy in America.* Trans. by Henry Reeve. 2 vols. New York: Co-operative Publication Society, 1900 (orig. 1835).

Tumin, Melvin M. *Desegregation: Resistance and Readiness.* Princeton: Princeton Univ. Press, 1958.

Turnbull, Colin. *The Forest People.* Garden City, N.Y.: Doubleday, 1962.

U.S. Congress. "Toward Economic Development for Native American Communities," prepared for the Joint Economic Committee by Helen W. Johnson. *American Indians in Rural Poverty* (Washington, D.C.: Government Printing Office, 1969), 19–45.

Warner, W. Lloyd, and J. Low. *Social System of the Modern Factory.* New Haven: Yale Univ. Press, 1941.

Warner, W. Lloyd and P. Lunt. *The Social Life of a Modern Community.* New Haven: Yale Univ. Press, 1941.

Warner, W. Lloyd and L. Srole. *The Social Systems of American Ethnic Groups.* New Haven: Yale Univ. Press, 1945.

Warner, W. Lloyd. *Democracy in Jonesville: A Study in Quality and Inequality.* New York: Harper, 1949.

Warner, W. Lloyd, *et al. Social Class in America.* Chicago: Social Science Research Associates, 1949.

Wax, Rosalie H. *Doing Fieldwork: Warnings and Advice.* Chicago: Univ. of Chicago Press, 1971.

Weber, Max. "Science As a Vocation," in *The Relevance of Sociology,* ed. Jack D. Douglas, 45–63. New York: Appleton, 1970.

Weppner, Robert S. "Urban Economic Opportunities: The Example of Denver."
    In *The American Indian in Urban Society,* eds. J. O. Waddell and Michael
    Watson, 245–73. Boston: Little, 1971.
West, James. *Plainville U.S.A.* New York: Columbia Univ. Press, 1945.
Whyte, William Foote. *Street Corner Society.* Chicago: Univ. of Chicago Press, 1955
    (orig. 1943).
Willey, Gordon R. *An Introduction to American Archaeology.* Englewood Cliffs,
    N.J.: Prentice-Hall, 1966.
Williams, Thomas Rhys. *Field Methods in the Study of Culture.* New York: Holt,
    1967.
Wissler, Clark. *Indians of the United States.* Garden City, N.Y.: Doubleday, 1940.

Index

Alien. *See* Foreigner

American Ethnological Society meeting, 83

Anthropologist, Asian: identity as, 95; lack of resentment to, 85; responses of Indians to, 70; responses of southerners to, 17, 20, 25; role-playing as, 41, 115. *See also* Field work, anthropological

Applied anthropology, 20, 22–23, 24, 137n; role of females in, 100

Arensberg, Conrad M., 42

Asians: cultural traits of, 70; epithet for, 46; expected role of, 13; prejudice against, 8, 47; receptiveness of Choctaws to, 83; responses of whites to, 96; special treatment of, 97; stereotype behavior of, 14, 52, 54, 124, 127; way of thinking, 66

Bailey, Wilfrid C., 135n

Bevier, Thomas, 141n

Blacks: attitudes of whites toward, 117, 128; attitudes toward other racial groups, 97, 130–31, 139n; family of, 120, 139n; job opportunities for, 130; life style of, 36; manner of speech of, 131; participation in local government of, 129–30; prejudice against, 8; racial perspectives toward, 108, 109, 121

Brandt, Vincent S.R., 15

Bryce, James, 16

Bureau of Indian Affairs (BIA), 89, 96, 101, 106–107

Burgess, Ernest W., 47

Cherokees, 69, 143n. *See also* Indians, American

Chickasaws, 114, 143. *See also* Indians, American

Chinese, 3, 17, 22, 96, 108

Choctaws: acculturation of, 89; associations with blacks and whites, 87; genealogy of, 90; iden-

Choctaws (*cont.*)

tity and cultural heritage of, 88–89, 114; kinship system of, 82, 88–91, 142n; legend of, 143n; marriages of, 87–88, 90; migration of, 81–82, 86–87, 91; off-reservation, 85, 90, 92; response to an Asian, 95; social, economic, and demographic study of, 85, 95, 111; in tri-ethnic setting, 75. *See also* Indians, American; Mississippi Band of Choctaw Indians

Deloria, Vine, Jr., 70, 113

Dollard, John, 48

Enculturation, 131

Ethnic group, 121

Ethnocentrism, 93

Ethnography, 126

Field researchers. *See* Field workers, anthropological

Field work, anthropological, 12, 23–24, 47, 79; in the American South, 13–15, 19, 81, 127; appearance and mode of dress used in, 27, 100; with blacks and whites, 16; with Choctaws, 16, 69, 71–72, 108, 111, 116, 132; intellectual tribute to, 68; preliminary stage of, 73; among pulpwood workers, 18–19, 29, 67; requirement for, 20; ritual in, 47; selecting a community for, 25; technical equipment used in, 29, 30, 32

Field workers, anthropological, 25, 29, 100. *See also* Field work, anthropological

Foreigner, 38, 54, 95; advantages of being a, 40, 52; assistance from natives to, 104; attitudes toward a, 124; special treatment of, 62–63; as a student, 9, 52

Forestry Abstract, 21

THE UNIVERSITY OF TENNESSEE PRESS
KNOXVILLE